JANE NOTTAGE is a writer and broadcaster, who contributes regularly to several national newspapers including the *Mail on Sunday* and the *Express*. Fluent in Italian, she has followed the fortunes of the Ferrari team for many years and worked with Luca di Montezemolo before he became Chairman of Ferrari in 1992. For three seasons Jane has been given unprecedented access to Formula One's most famous team. She has written five books, including *Venables' England: The Making of the Team* and *Gleneagles*.

*This book is dedicated to Paul Wiget,
with thanks for four wonderful years and
with much love for a very happy future for
him and his four lovely children,
Phil, Isobel, Kevin and Anna, and Phil's
beautiful girlfriend Anette.*

Ferrari

THE PASSION AND THE PAIN

Jane Nottage

CollinsWillow
An Imprint of HarperCollinsPublishers

First published in hardback in 1997 by
CollinsWillow, an imprint of HarperCollins*Publishers*,
London

Revised paperback edition published in 1998

© Jane Nottage 1998

1 3 5 7 9 8 6 4 2

A CIP catalogue record for this book is available
from the British Library

ISBN 0 00 218887 2

Origination by Dot Gradations, Essex, UK
Printed and bound by
Caledonian International Book Manufacturing, Glasgow

Contents

Foreword
by NIKI LAUDA

Winning one World Championship with Ferrari is a special feeling. Winning two is simply unforgettable. Enzo Ferrari, like his cars, came out of a unique mould. He was sometimes difficult and intransigent, but above all he was the driving force behind one of the greatest racing teams of all time. We had some memorable run-ins during my four years at Ferrari, but my respect for this giant of motor racing and what he accomplished eclipses all else. Having later started my own company, Lauda Air, I understand the effort required to build up and maintain a successful business.

There are many good memories from my time as a Ferrari driver, but one or two are outstanding, such as the first time I won a Grand Prix with Ferrari. It happened at Jarama (in Spain) in 1974 and after this I understood what it was like to feel the warmth of the passionate *tifosi*, who were overjoyed.

Winning my first Formula One Drivers' Championship with Ferrari was one of the highlights of my life. When it actually happened everything seemed to go by in a flash – the celebrations, the victory dinner, meeting the fans. But at the end I was left with an intense feeling of happiness, which I will never forget.

I was fortunate enough to have Luca di Montezemolo as my team manager when I won that title in 1975. As well as a being colleague, Luca became a friend and when he returned to Ferrari in 1992 as chairman, I became a consultant to help rebuild the fortunes of the team.

Luca is a brilliant strategist and visionary. He recognized the need to employ the right people in the right places, and over the last six years he has done just that. The result is that the Ferrari Formula One team has been able to show in the last two years particularly that it is once again a serious contender for the Formula One World Constructors' Championship.

That kind of action takes courage and perseverance, particularly in a company like Ferrari, which is quintessentially Italian in its approach and its methods. Politics and intrigue have always played a part in the management, and it isn't easy to cut through that and prepare the company for the future. To that end Luca has done a brilliant job, as have all the members of the team – especially Team Director Jean Todt and Michael Schumacher, who is the best racing driver of his generation, and the talented and competitive Eddie Irvine.

Above all, one must never forget that Ferrari is a team made up of different nationalities and personalities, and each and every one of them plays an important role. A racing team works under constant pressure, so the most junior mechanic is as important as the most senior manager in that they must all execute their jobs efficiently and quickly.

This book is unique in that it offers the reader a glimpse of what life is really like working for one of the most glamorous and enigmatic teams in Grand Prix motor racing; and, for the very first time, the sweat and toil and the passion and the pain of being part of Ferrari can be observed at close quarters.

Niki Lauda, Vienna, 1998

Introduction

The sound is unmistakable. A deep throaty roar leading to a high-pitched whine. It's another day, another country and the millionaire boys are playing with their favourite toys. Round and round they go, darting in and out like multi-coloured insects engaged in some ancient ritualistic dance.

Bearing the names of their sponsors like proud warriors they automatically draw attention from the small groups gathered on the slopes overlooking the circuit. National flags wave in the breeze and the onlookers express their delight as their favourite drivers pass by. The cars in their distinct livery, each driver locked in his own private race to go ever faster, dance over the tarmac – gold, grey, black, white with a tartan strip and light blue.

The circus continues, and then from the distant pits another sound is heard and the crowd stirs in eager anticipation. A guttural battle cry is followed by a roar of power as the V10 engine propels the car down the pit lane and onto the glistening track. A flash of scarlet as the founder member of Formula One motor racing joins the rest. Anticipation changes to raw passion, and the fans erupt at the sight and sound of the bright red car driven by the supreme warrior himself.

Michael Schumacher is in a Ferrari. Individually enticing, together they are an unbeatable combination of power and emotion. The brilliant German driver in the car that stirs the heart. Among a family of beauties the Ferrari stands head and shoulders above the others. And not just in Formula One. From the boardrooms of Manhattan to the deserts of Africa, owning a Ferrari is the embodiment of many people's hopes and dreams, something that represents escape, beauty and the good life. It has also transcended the role of being a mere form of transport and become a focus for the emotions of the whole Italian nation. When Ferrari does well the nation dances, when Ferrari does badly the nation cries.

But what is it like to carry the hopes of a nation? To be responsible for the intangible feelings that ebb and flow around the stable of the prancing horse?

Fast forward to 1998. Dateline: 13 September. Place: Monza, home ground of the famous and fanatical *tifosi*. The scarlet cars screech past the chequered flag, first and second. Schumacher stands on the top step of the podium, Irvine on the next step down. The crowd and the team are delirious. The magical result, not seen at Ferrari in recent history on their home ground, has revitalized everyone involved. It is the sum total of the determination, effort and skill of so many people, and now everyone can rejoice that the hard work has paid off: Schumacher is back in the contest for the 1998 World Drivers' Championship; and Ferrari are challenging once again for the Constructors' title. Of course, as history was to decree at the climax of the season in Japan, it would be the runners-up spot yet again for Ferrari and their German wünderkind. But for now, the glory of Monza was something to behold.

At the end of three progressive seasons, the Ferrari renaissance is well underway. Plots and counter-plots are long forgotten. The pace and reliability of a small red car is what matters. Ferrari might make Machiavelli seem like an innocent but it is the only company to have perpetrated the myth of desire for 50 years, the only Formula One team that attracts a passionate, committed army of supporters throughout the world.

We stand on the threshold of a new millennium and we are

still transfixed by the power and emotion generated by the need to feel we can be a part of Ferrari, maybe even one day drive one of their cars. We need to be a part of the dream even if, for some of us, that dream is as elusive as scaling Mount Everest. If the emotion is strong on the outside, what is it like on the inside? Let's take a journey into the heart of the stable of the prancing horse and find out.

Jane Nottage, London, 1998

CHAPTER ONE

The Legend Lives On

'Ferrari is motor racing. It is the representation of everything motor racing stands for – speed, glamour, style and excitement.'

Bernie Ecclestone
FOCA President

Once upon a time there lived a man called Enzo Ferrari. He produced beautiful cars, won many World Championships, built a company that became famous throughout the world, resided in a lovely place called Maranello, where the sun always shone and he lived happily ever after. Fairy stories. Wonderful aren't they? They allow people to dream of a better world and believe that everything is always beautiful. The heroes are always good looking and the future is always full of hope and happiness. Not unlike life at Ferrari, or so most people would have us believe. Over the years the legend has been carefully constructed and perpetuated by the people at the stable of the black prancing horse, to make us believe that Ferrari is the ultimate dream, the legend that delivers your fantasies.

Even the famous emblem is shrouded in mystery. Folklore has it that Enzo Ferrari was enjoying success as an Alfa Romeo driver, when after yet another victorious race a man pushed his way through the crowd that had gathered round the winner, shook Enzo's hand warmly and invited him back to his house so he could make a presentation. This man was the father of famous World War I flying ace, Francesco Baracca, who had shot down 35 adversaries before his life ended in 1918. As his personal badge, Baracca had used a black prancing horse. After his demise, his family was sent the prancing horse symbol on a piece of aeroplane fabric and it was their wish that this famous emblem should be passed on to Enzo Ferrari in recognition of his courage and talent on the race track.

There is no doubt that Enzo Ferrari was a remarkable man. In 1947 he started to produce and sell road cars to enable him to finance his racing career. He was perceptive enough to realize that if he created exclusivity there would be more demand than supply and so he built up a company that today, as we stand on the threshold of the next millennium, is still the marque that most people dream of owning and driving. He also created a Formula One racing team that has become a legend within the rarefied world of motor racing. Ferrari is a name that is synonymous with glamour, style and power.

However, being a genius who built up an empire from nothing didn't necessarily make Enzo a wonderful person. People seem to link the two, but most really successful businessmen are single minded, despotic and completely egocentric. Enzo Ferrari was no different. He often treated staff like servants, enjoying his absolute power as leader. He kept racing drivers in their place (bearing in mind the over-inflated egos of some of today's drivers, many would list that as a positive characteristic) and he was hardly a New Man. His wife cannot have had an easy time being married to a legend. He built a house on his test circuit so he could be near to his first love, racing, and know exactly what was going on both with the car and with the team. He fathered an illegitimate child, Piero Lardi, whom he welcomed into the business after his own son died. His wife, naturally, as was the tradition of the times, would have been expected to put up with it all, plus have his dinner ready when he wanted it. He was demanding, selfish and authoritarian, but nevertheless a brilliant man, and in spite of – or maybe because of – his faults, he is always remembered with great affection by people who knew him.

Niki Lauda, who won two World Championships with Ferrari, recalls Enzo Ferrari as a man of extraordinary influence and recounts the strength and mystique surrounding the Ferrari legend. 'Ferrari has something extra,' he says. 'It's something indefinable and unique, and every time I walked through the doors of the factory at Maranello or stepped into the car, I felt the added importance of being that unique thing – a Ferrari driver. There was, is and always will be a special place in my heart that is reserved for Ferrari.'

Jody Scheckter was also 'that unique thing' and won the World Championship for Ferrari in 1979 – the last driver to do so. 'I think for any driver of any ability to drive for Ferrari is a dream come true,' he says. 'It is still the most historic marque in motor racing. The magic of driving for Ferrari is that you're driving for the whole of Italy, not just the team.' Nigel Mansell, the last Englishman to drive for Ferrari, says, 'Driving for Ferrari offers a very special experience. They are true thoroughbred racers, they only want to win and for me the reality was very similar to the dream.'

SHEER POWER
FERRARI HAS ALWAYS BEEN A MAJOR FORCE IN FIA

Behind the romantic mystique and glamour of Ferrari lies sheer, raw power. Formula One is a breeding ground for power but Ferrari is the master. Max Mosley, President of FIA (Fédération Internationale de l'Automobile, the sport's governing body based in Paris) explains how Ferrari entered the inner sanctum of Formula One and became the main power broker. 'Politically, Ferrari has always been a major force in FIA. Until the emergence of British racing in the 1960s, all decisions were made somewhere between Paris and Turin. It was just a question of which year and where the centre of gravity was. The Concorde Agreement (the Maastricht treaty of Formula One) was drawn up in 1980 and 1981, and it has a provision that when Formula One matters are discussed the vote of the President of the Manufacturer's Commission would be exercised by a representative from the legalist's side. The legalists were one of two factions which formed in the late 70s and early 80s. It was basically Ferrari, Renault and Alfa

Romeo, and the other faction was us, together with the FOCA [Formula One Constructors' Association] teams.

'FOCA had a seat on the World Council, and we found a compromise whereby in addition to Formula One having a seat on the World Council, another person who is President of the Manufacturers' Commission has a seat. He represents the World's Motor Industry, the big manufacturers. When Formula One matters were discussed, the legalists had their representative and historically this has always been Ferrari.'

Ferrari, in typical Latin fashion, has always been alert to the most imperceptible political currents, and it was this talent that kept it in the thick of things. As Mosley says, 'In the 70s, when FOCA became powerful, we ended up with FOCA on one side and FIA/FISA on the other, with Ferrari as the fulcrum. It would move a little bit one way and then a little bit the other way, influencing the decisions. Enzo Ferrari was an absolute master of that sort of politics. He wanted to make sure Formula One succeeded, so he nearly always backed Bernie [Ecclestone], as he realized that Bernie was going to make Formula One into something big. However, by moving a bit towards the governing body he could obtain a more favourable position in negotiations, which was a very wise move. Now all the relationships between me, Bernie and Ferrari are very solid.'

So what if, for argument's sake, someone stood up and said: 'Well, Williams should be our representative as it has been the most successful team in the last five years,' or 'McLaren because it dominated the 80s'? What would happen?

Mosley smiles before replying with certainty. 'Nothing would happen. It would stay as it is. Ferrari has got one overwhelming advantage and that is it was there on 13 May 1950 (the first Formula One World Championship race) and has continued to be there, and even when it wasn't winning it has been a tremendous part of Formula One. Now it is right up at the top again. As Chairman Mao said, "Power comes from the barrel of a gun" – although in the case of Formula One power comes from success. If you're successful and have got tradition, your political position is very strong.'

Mosley also has first-hand experience of Enzo Ferrari's schoolboy humour. 'Twice a year all the teams and everyone would go down to visit Ferrari, and we'd all have lunch together. Enzo would always sit Bernie next to him, and when Bernie wasn't looking he'd slip a large piece of Parmesan cheese on his plate. According to the old man, Parmesan has aphrodisiac qualities, and he'd always say without fail "that will get the little man going". It always made him crack up right to the end of his life.'

A clever man with a keen nose for politics, Mosley freely admits to being completely seduced by Ferrari. 'If someone said to me you can have any job in motorsport, I'd choose to run Ferrari. I quite envy Luca [di Montezemolo, the present chairman] his job. I know it would be challenging and difficult, but then all the top jobs are. I have no doubt that it would certainly be the most interesting.'

Bernie Ecclestone, the President of the Formula One Constructors' Association (FOCA), is the man who has made Formula One an exciting, visually entertaining sport and a business that is a commercial success. Having known Enzo Ferrari so well, he fondly remembers the old man, and Bernie's trepidation at what might happen after his death in 1988.

'I have many happy, personal memories of Ferrari as I had a long friendship with the great Enzo, who was always supportive of all I did. When he died I missed him on a personal level, and I also wondered what would happen to

Ferrari and if it would continue in the same way. I am delighted to see that the team has followed in the footsteps of tradition and is being run in the same way by the right people, who will ensure that it grows and develops as we enter the next millennium and the 21st century.'

INTO THE FUTURE
GRADUALLY THINGS STARTED TO IMPROVE

The death of the great Enzo Ferrari in 1988 was the end of an era at Ferrari. He had been the creator and motivating force of the car company for over 40 years and now, finally, it was time to take stock and move on towards the 21st century.

When Chief Designer John Barnard left Ferrari for the first time at the end of 1989, Alain Prost nearly won the World Championship the following year in 1990 before the famous coming together with Ayrton Senna at Suzuka effectively lost Prost the Championship.

This prompted Ferrari to appoint a new heir not only to take over the running of the company but also to lead it into the new millennium. The new messiah was Luca di Montezemolo, one of Italy's brightest international businessmen, who had already achieved success at Ferrari when he was team manager at the time Niki Lauda won two World Championships (1975 and 1977). Early on in his career, Montezemolo had been earmarked for great things by his mentor, Fiat boss Gianni Agnelli and he had moved through the ranks at Fiat. He had also been head of the organizing committee for the football World Cup held in Italy in 1990, before he had been offered the top job at Ferrari in 1992.

As well as being bright and vastly experienced in the realms of international marketing and commerce, Montezemolo was aware of the tradition and history so integral to Ferrari. He was therefore ideally placed to lead the company. It was to be a quiet and dignified revolution as opposed to an outright battle.

Montezemolo's strategy was to get the best people in the top positions to enable the Formula One team to start winning again after a disappointing 1991 season. One of his first moves was to recapture award-winning designer John Barnard to prepare a competitive car.

Barnard re-joined his old stable on 1 August 1992, and took up the challenge of getting involved in a team that was on the edge of a new renaissance. Like many clever, successful men he was seduced by the thought of getting it right at one of the most difficult, disparate teams in Formula One, and he had enough self-confidence to think he could pull it off. In theory it should have been a happy union between a large budget and a well respected talent. But for the Ferrari–Barnard association to be truly happy it would need serenity, patience and total commitment on both parts and that wasn't going to be easy.

It started off full of golden promise. Barnard had to gather a new team to work at the new offices in Shalford, Guildford that would effectively be the design centre (Ferrari Design and Development – FDD) for Ferrari Formula One cars. At the same time he was under pressure to produce a new car for 1993. 'We agreed that I would take an overview and get things up and running. But within days of signing the contract, I was being asked how quickly I could do a new car. I hadn't even got a building to work from...'

Having secured a slightly cynical but nevertheless brilliant designer and parked him in England to get on and design a new car, Montezemolo continued with his search for the right people. Previous Technical Director Harvey Postlethwaite had been persuaded to return. 'The first time was wonderful, when

I was working for the old man [Enzo Ferrari]. He could be difficult but everyone knew where they stood and he kept it all together by ruling with a rod of iron. The second time was awful. On my first day back in 1992, I realized I had made an awful mistake in being persuaded to return. There was no direction and things changed every five minutes. It was the start of two truly awful years and I couldn't wait to get out. I used to keep a piece of paper with my salary written on it in the top drawer of my desk; when things got really rough, I would open the drawer, look at the figure and remember the reason I had returned!' Postlethwaite sums up his feelings by declaring, 'Ferrari is like a film star with halitosis – from afar it looks glamorous and seductive, but get near and it poisons you.'

Next on Montezemola's shopping list was Frenchman Jean Todt. Todt is an exceptionally gifted team manager, having led Peugeot to several World Championship titles in sportscars after a successful career as a rally co-driver. He was enjoying his job at Peugeot but wanted the ultimate challenge of Formula One, and when Peugeot declined to compete at that level, he was ready to try new pastures.

A small, Napoleonic character with a severe countenance but an understanding heart, the job of team principal at Ferrari was one challenge Todt was determined to see through to the end and achieve his objectives of bringing structure and organization to a team that sorely needed it.

Team Co-ordinator Nigel Stepney was one of the first to feel the benefit of Todt's talents. He recalls how he joined Ferrari and the pre- and post-Todt periods. 'I joined in 1992 and it was the realization of a dream. I had worked with various English teams from 1978, and everyone warned me against going to work for Ferrari.

'They said, "It's big, it's political, you won't survive." After that, Ferrari became my number one choice. I love a challenge and it was a personal challenge for me. I thought I'd show a few people what I could do.

'When I walked through the door, it was like everyone said it was; it was like being thrown into the lion's den. Harvey Postlethwaite was in charge on the technical side and he put me in a "non" position, so I was there but not there. Once I got through the first year, things got better. The job evolved and I wanted to succeed, so I made it work. But what really turned it round for me was the arrival of Jean Todt at Ferrari at Magny-Cours [for the French Grand Prix] in 1993. When he arrived the whole structure of the place started to change. He picked me up and put me into a position, that of team co-ordinator, with which I knew and could grow. Jean Todt is brilliant at restructuring, and good at giving you support and confidence. If he trusts you and believes in you, he'll give you support and make you feel strong. That was vital at Ferrari.

'Before his arrival, it was very easy to feel insecure. Everyone was constantly trying to make you feel insecure, as they were insecure themselves. You expected the knife in your back at any moment. It was like Julius Caesar every day here. The Italians used to bunch together and it was difficult to fit into that structure. But with Todt's arrival a lot of people were able to start work and have definite responsibilities. It was like a breath of fresh air.'

Gradually things started to improve as Montezemolo created a strategy that was designed to put Ferrari back at the top, where it belonged. But it was to be another year before Ferrari took the last step in its renaissance and employed a World Champion as its driver.

Gerhard Berger and Jean Alesi were the Ferrari drivers at this time and were competent and talented, but their constant bickering did not help the team. The arrival of double World Champion Michael Schumacher from Benetton would change all that.

When Schumacher won his first World Championship in 1994, he dedicated it to Ayrton Senna, 'the man who should have won it'. Strangely enough, it should have been Senna who joined Ferrari in 1996, not Schumacher. Former Ferrari Press Officer Giancarlo Baccini says, 'Senna had always wanted to drive for Ferrari. Before he went to Williams he came and talked to us. We told him we weren't ready for him. We just weren't able to provide him with the car and facilities he needed. He was brilliant but also demanding and it would have broken the team to have a champion at that time. We told him to wait for a couple of years and then we would be ready. That would have been the 1996 season. He agreed and we continued to rebuild the team. But destiny decreed otherwise. That is not to say Schumacher was second choice. He is absolutely a world-class driver, and who knows if Senna would have joined us or not. The initial discussions with Senna were before Schumacher won his first World Championship and emerged as one of the all-time greats.'

The arrival of the brilliant German driver was almost the final piece of the jigsaw in the rebuilding of the team (Ross Brawn would arrive as technical director in December of 1996 and Rory Byrne as chief designer in January 1997). Montezemolo chose the moment carefully before taking on a driver who would demand the best in everything, and was also capable of giving the best.

At the launch of the 1996 car, the energetic Italian was full of optimism and determination. 'Just as a football team doesn't

MARANELLO: HOME TO FERRARI

In Maranello, it is impossible to escape the influence of Ferrari. No one is untouched, and Maranello has become like an extended family of the high-profile car company. When the prancing horse is unwell, the whole town is quiet and subdued, but when it is first past the winning post, the crescendo of noisy celebration is deafening.

The Ferrari factory straddles the main road and is as much a part of the Italian way of life as eating and praying. In fact much of Ferrari's history and tradition is centred on two restaurants: Il Cavallino and Il Montana. Enzo Ferrari had his own room at Il Cavallino, where he could entertain in privacy (a tradition that is handed down to every chairman) and Il Montana was host to the drivers when they came to town. The walls are littered with signed photographs and pieces of paper from the sons of Ferrari, those drivers and personnel who all became part of the legend.

expect to win a major title immediately the team restructures, we have the same philosophy of making steady progress towards our target of winning the World Championship.

'Three years ago we were two seconds off the pace of the best cars; now we are up among the best. By having Schumacher as our Number One driver we are demonstrating to the world that we are prepared to do everything possible to win. Also we feel ready to make the final leap to success. If we didn't feel ready, then we wouldn't have brought the best driver in the world into the team.'

A double World Champion at only 26 years of age, Schumacher was emerging as one of the best drivers of his generation. Ferrari knew it would have to pay for the best, and did so to the tune of $25 million. But as John Barnard says, 'When Ferrari signed Schumacher it was like they opened another piggy bank. Suddenly money was no object. You need a new machine? Buy it. Expand, employ the people you need and so on. It was a surprise as for the last three years we'd been told to hang tight, cut back, think before spending any extra money. Suddenly all that changed.'

Fortunately, when he met the press for the first time as a Ferrari driver, Schumacher didn't repeat the mistake he made in his first press conference. When asked what his father did, he replied with a straight face, 'He likes screwing.' For once, the hacks were rendered speechless, until it was explained that in German a screw is a carpenter, someone who likes playing around with wood!

THE FINAL PIECES
ON 15 FEBRUARY 1996 THE NEW FERRARI F1 CAR WAS UNVEILED

Another vital ingredient to the rebuilding of Ferrari was the return of Shell as a Ferrari partner, along with fellow sponsors Philip Morris, Asprey, Magneti Marelli, Telecom Italia, Goodyear and Pioneer.

The red hot passion of Ferrari combined with the cool, clinical, technical expertise of Shell is a forceful combination. Fuels and lubricants are a vital aspect of improving performance. In-depth research and development at the Shell Research and Technology Centre at Thornton in Cheshire, has led to a far more efficient and powerful engine. The engine was to be an important factor in Ferrari's return to the top.

Completing the dawn of a new era for the Italian car giants, on 15 February 1996 the new Ferrari Formula One car was unveiled and presented to the international media. More than half a million people logged on to the Internet to follow the presentation ceremony. There was much hope and optimism that finally the tide was turning in favour of the stable of the prancing horse.

● ● ●

The passion of winning, the pain of losing. Ferrari has known both. But what is it about the red racers that continues to entice and seduce? Above all, what is it like to be a part of the team that is part of Formula One folklore? Let's take a journey through the Schumacher era, 1996-98, and find out.

CHAPTER TWO

On a Wing
and a Prayer

'I'm not harder on the team than I am on myself.

If I make a mistake, I kick myself.'

Michael Schumacher
after the 1996 Argentinian GP

Despite the atmosphere of hope and optimism that surrounded the presentation of Ferrari's new F1 car on 15 February 1996, there were many crossed fingers as well. The car was late, very late, partly because the development of the previous season's car was still being carried out in England rather than at Maranello. Because of a shortage of staff, Ferrari Design and Development (FDD) had not put that development down early enough to get on with the new car. A major concern for Ferrari was that there was hardly any time to test before the season's first race in Melbourne on 10 March.

Chief Designer John Barnard has been criticized for being removed from the realities of modern Formula One racing. It is an accusation that he is keen to dismiss. 'I only have one problem and that is that everyone expects me to produce something new and take the next step. If I don't do that they just say it is only another Formula One car, he must be finished. I push hard to find something new, but the realities of modern Formula One racing are quite simple: if you want to win and be in the top group, you need more than 200 people, a sizeable budget and a good engine. There is no way of cutting corners. You have to build up to that point.'

At Fiorano, the Ferrari test track just outside Maranello, a problem emerged involving slight cracks in the gearbox bellhousing which caused an oil leak, and the team decided to go to Estoril in Portugal to try and rectify the situation. It was the start of many sleepless nights for the Ferrari Team Manager, Claudio Berro – the person responsible for shifting men and machines around the world and ensuring that everything arrives on time in one piece. He also has to ensure that the team has acceptable accommodation and transport, and that team personnel are warm and comfortable while they are away from the factory. Additionally, he liaises with the motor racing authorities, FIA and FOCA, and attends meetings with Team Director, Jean Todt.

It might seem like a job from heaven − constant travel, exotic locations, five-star hotels, the chance to meet beautiful, rich people and have a good time, plus the glamour of being part of Ferrari. However, on a wet, freezing cold, fog-infested morning in the middle of northern Italy, glamour and having a good time were far from Berro's thoughts. His immediate problem was how to transport the race cars, the team and the accompanying equipment to Portugal for the hastily arranged test, and be ready to meet the departure schedule for Australia, the country hosting the first round of the FIA Formula One World Championship for 1996. (The team was due to leave on an Alitalia flight bound for Melbourne at 12.30 pm on Friday 1 March.)

It was quickly apparent that the team couldn't travel as it normally does by road; it would have taken five days for a trip to Estoril and back. A quick alternative was needed − and needed fast. It required a cool head and plenty of stamina to put it all together. Fortunately, Berro is calm by nature, and solves problems in a logical and efficient manner. 'I investigated the possibility of renting an aircraft, and found a Russian Antonov plane for the cars and equipment and a jet for all the technicians. I asked for detailed measurements of the Russian aircraft as I had to be absolutely sure that everything would fit in. We had six or seven cases of small spare parts as well as crates of larger spare parts and the racing car.

'This was the start of 10 sleepless nights for me. The cars were at the test track at Fiorano until the afternoon, then they were transported to Bologna and the plane took off at 3 am. It landed at 6 am, and I was constantly on the phone to check and double-check that everything was going according to plan. I had an aircraft on standby for two days, for which we had to pay a penalty, but we had to be sure we could take off at short notice. We had a combination of cars moving between Fiorano and Estoril. We had trucks to transport them from the airport at Lisbon to the track. I also had to make sure the technicians arrived, and so it was a hectic and complex period. All in all, it was the most difficult part of the year.'

Against this background of uncertainty, it was with understandable trepidation that the team arrived in Melbourne. Berro, however, was the most relaxed. 'As soon as I boarded the plane I fell asleep and slept for a solid 24 hours. I stepped off the plane feeling great. Everyone had jet lag, but I didn't. I told them the solution is to avoid sleep before the trip. That wasn't a popular suggestion!'

Berro saved the day and enabled Jean Todt and his team to get on with the job of fixing the car. Berro had worked closely with Todt at Peugeot, from the time they were rally co-drivers to their individual rises through the ranks which saw Todt as the overall boss and Berro as director of sport for Peugeot in Italy. The two men have an almost telepathic understanding, which is necessary when working in the hot cauldron of pressure that is Maranello.

As the Italian population slept unaware that Ferrari racing cars were shooting backwards and forwards across the airways, Berro's team members were already checking and re-checking arrangements for later in the year. Miodrag Kotur, Pino Gozzo and Massimo Balocchi make up the logistics group. They oversee the movement of the trucks, team personnel, and equipment round the world. Giuseppe Gozzo, Pino to his friends, is the man at the track who has the sometimes difficult – if not impossible – job of making sure all the travel arrangements run smoothly. When things go wrong he has to put them right. It is a job where the saying 'it's not what you know, but who you know' comes to the fore. When team personnel want to change their flights and travel arrangements during a period where the aircraft are overbooked, Pino has to use his wide range of contacts to pull strings and make sure that people get to their destinations on time.

THE SEASON BEGINS
IRVINE'S THIRD PLACE IN AUSTRALIA WAS A BONUS

And so the team arrived in Melbourne, albeit feeling far from confident. But everyone was in for a pleasant surprise. Things were not quite as bad as they thought. They had feared being right off the pace and a long way down the grid or, even worse, being unreliable and only lasting a few laps. But they put on a good show, even though there were problems.

Williams, as predicted, outshone everyone, with Jacques Villeneuve and Damon Hill on pole position and second respectively. But Ferrari did well: Michael Schumacher qualified fourth and his team-mate Eddie Irvine started third on the grid.

For Chief Engineer Giorgio Ascanelli, the team really was living on a wing and a prayer in Australia. Ascanelli is in charge of the team at the race track; he talks to the drivers and their race engineers about race strategy and set-up, but ultimately it is his decision. He is responsible for directing the whole operation and so he has the weight of Italian hopes and fears placed squarely on his shoulders. He is an emotional, volatile character but is also strong and direct which helps him to cope.

Ascanelli doesn't mince words or suffer fools gladly. As he

says, 'Leading a team of people is more difficult than managing objects. In Formula One speed is essential and there isn't time for diplomacy and politics. The pressure on Ferrari is greater than in other teams as the success of Ferrari has an effect on every aspect of Italian life, including the government and the humour of the people. When the Italian football team won the 1982 World Cup, it gave the Italian people and the economy a real lift.'

Like most of his colleagues at Ferrari, Ascanelli is a fervent believer in stability. 'It has been difficult for people to come in after Enzo Ferrari and we have struggled to maintain some sort of stability. Williams has become strong through building up a team that can work together. Its team doesn't change much from year to year. I believe stability is very important. There is an intrinsic amount of information in a person's head and because we are all so busy we just don't have time to pass everything on to a new person.'

Race strategy and set-up is a complex business. The first is as much about outfoxing your opponents as taking external elements into consideration; the latter is based on many different factors: aerodynamics, engine mechanics and tyres, for example. Then there is the question of driver style. A lot of drivers have to work at being quick, but for Michael Schumacher it just comes naturally, so it allows him to release a lot of mental power on thinking about the race. 'However,' says John Barnard, 'where Schumacher really scores is that he has the ability to impress a calmness on the team even when things aren't going well.

Schumacher is, of course, not without his weaknesses, and like many people the things that make him brilliant can also work against him. His determined, focused approach is helping Ferrari to concentrate its resources and work out problems, but he doesn't take on new ideas very easily. Barnard laughs as he says, 'If you can explain things logically to him, he'll take it on board, but if it is a hunch, getting him to change is like turning the *Queen Mary*. It's not easy.'

In 1996 Ferrari was already struggling with a completely new car. In Australia the main problem was the unexpected cracking of the titanium gearbox casing. Shell, Ferrari's technical partner, detected traces of titanium when the lubricant was analysed. It was an unpleasant surprise. Barnard says, 'We had been running the engine in a hybrid version of last year's car and we hadn't seen that happening. We think the engine is vibrating badly, causing the cracking. It is the first time we've used a V10; we ran using a titanium gearbox behind a V12 in 1994, and we didn't have these problems.'

There was also contention over the re-design of the cockpit area. Some teams felt that Williams and Jordan had not kept to the spirit of the new regulations drawn up to give drivers extra protection and were therefore gaining an aerodynamic advantage over other teams. Ferrari, like many others, had designed a high-sided cockpit.

Overall, the car was proving to be very difficult in terms of drivability. Irvine's third place in Australia was a bonus, but the team returned to Maranello with a lot of work to do in the ten days before departing for the South American circuits. The races in Brazil and Argentina were not only long distance but also 'back to back' (a week apart), and the old gearbox had to be fitted in the car. Unfortunately, it isn't as easy as simply replacing the new with the old. As Ascanelli says, 'We knew there was a hell of a lot of work to do between Australia and South America. We had to have a new water system, do electrical work, bodywork, a new starter motor ... and we had ten days to do it in.'

BRAZIL AND ARGENTINA
THINGS WENT FROM BAD TO WORSE

The team went to South America feeling unhappy – and things went from bad to worse. Ascanelli says of Brazil, 'The São Paolo circuit is very bumpy and doesn't suit our car. We had to just limit the damage, and wait until we could get back in the wind tunnel and do the necessary work to improve the car. The race went worse than I expected. After two days of sunshine, I was writing the race preparation report with ten minutes to go before the pit lane opened, when I looked up and saw it was raining. Disaster! There was no time to alter the fuel level, and our two-stop strategy which was good for the dry was not good for the wet, where we would have been better with one stop.'

Schumacher demonstrated his class and pulled off the impossible by bringing the car in third. His calm approach was paying dividends and he refused to get caught up in any hysteria. 'I am enjoying driving for Ferrari. It is a challenge and I wanted a challenge. I am paid to work, not be on holiday. The car will be in the wind tunnel for the whole of April and we will be working hard to alleviate the problems. The car was worse than in Melbourne, we seem to be losing power everywhere, but the V10 engine shows good potential.'

The V10 engine was proving to be a good move. As Barnard says, 'I promoted moving from a V12 to a V10 engine for a long time. When Jean Todt arrived it made things easier, as he was also a fan of the V10. You have to pay a heavy penalty for the V12 in terms of the overall package. The cooling requirements for the V12 are very big; it is longer, it is heavy and it is fuel thirsty. Offsetting these negative aspects was the fact that the V12 should have a higher top-end power than the V10. However, I was always a bit dubious about this. Now we have the V10 we can see this is true. After limited development the V10 is proving to have nearly as good top-end power as the V12. The negative side of the V10 is the vibration problem, which seems to lead to the gearbox cracking. We are investigating this further.'

The next race was in Buenos Aires over the Easter weekend, but there were to be no celebrations for the two Ferrari drivers. Schumacher qualified in second place for the race, with Irvine 10th. Irvine brought the car home in fifth place, to gain two valuable points, but Schumacher was forced to retire when a piece of debris from another car hit his rear wing.

Even though we were only three races into the new season, the rumours were flying around as speculation mounted that Ferrari was going to build a new car to take the team through the rest of the season. Jean Todt remained firm and publicly stated, 'We need more time testing before we can make a decision.' Privately, he was less convinced declaring, 'I'm not happy, I'll only be happy when we win.'

The atmosphere was muted as everyone left South America and headed back to Europe. They had survived the first three races, but only just. The first European race of the season was at the Nurburgring in Germany and the fans would be out in force. Publicly, Schumacher was remaining calm; privately it was another matter. As Nigel Stepney says, 'Schumacher doesn't wash his dirty linen in public as our previous drivers did. He can give shit behind closed doors, but he does it in private, which is much better because if everyone knows our problems, they know our weaknesses. There is a much better atmosphere than last year. There will always be pressure on us, but it is more contained. If we lose a wheel nut in a race, the media will analyse it forever, but if Williams lose a wheel nut they are not put under a microscope like us. The difference is that now we look at the problem and rectify it with the minimum of fuss. That is a big step forward.'

Schumacher says, 'There's no point in criticising the team in public. I work with the guys and they all try to do their best. If we feel there should be some improvements then we have to discuss it between ourselves. I don't think I'm particularly hard. If I notice a mistake, then I will point it out and try to improve it. I'm not harder on the team than I am on myself. If I make a mistake, I kick myself. You shouldn't make a difference between how you treat others and how you treat yourself.'

Added to the problems of the South American races was a big prang that occured in Argentina, albeit after the race. Claudio Berro explains, 'When I was sitting on the pit wall during practice, I looked at the start lights and registered that they seemed to be hanging lower than normal. Then it went out of my mind until the day after the race. The trucks arrived to take the cars to the airport, loaded them on and drove out of the circuit. There was a horrible crash and it was proved that the lights had been lower than normal, about four metres lower in fact. The result was they'd hit our cars on the trucks. Eddie Irvine's car had been smashed, the suspension had been damaged and it had been pushed backwards into the spare car, which was loaded behind it. About 200 million lire's worth of damage was done. That was all we needed with the work we had to do on the cars anyway.'

Work, work, work. There was a never ending list of modifications needed. When Schumacher was asked to discuss the improvements required on the car, his reply was to the point. 'This press conference is too short!' There was also another reason to feel nervous. Schumacher had received a death threat in the form of a letter claiming to come from a national liberation group, sent to two Belgian newspapers. It said that the terrorist organization would kill German Chancellor Helmut Kohl, Foreign Minister Klaus Kinkel... and Michael Schumacher.

BACK IN EUROPE
JEAN TODT'S THOUGHTS WERE ON HIS FUTURE

The beginning of the European season brought some respite for Ferrari. It is easier to work on the car nearer to home and also easier to transport equipment. In addition, more VIP visitors and new team members join the circuit.

The new press centre motorhome made its debut at the Nurburgring for the fourth race of the season. Shiny, bright red and constantly preened and polished, it is a focal point in the paddock and a home for the official team press conferences, as well as for guests.

In terms of the racing, Schumacher was second fastest on the Friday (even with, or maybe because of, an out of sorts stomach!), with Irvine wallowing down in 15th place. The cars were now fitted with the 1996 gearbox and a few new aerodynamic modifications after testing at Mugello (in Italy). Irvine's car suffered a misfire, which remained a puzzle until a few laps before the end of the session. He was also suffering from a lack of testing. Most, if not all, testing had been done by the Number One driver, and it hasn't been easy for the Ulsterman to sit back and watch. He has, to his credit, accepted his lot with his usual dark, dry humour. When asked how he coped with Schumacher's supreme fitness, Irvine remarked, 'I just call him up, ask him how many press-ups he's done, then ask him to do a few for me.'

Schumacher was, once again, cautious about his prospects for the race. 'I have tried many different solutions and although the car is quite good I did not manage to get it perfectly balanced. I will try and improve tomorrow [at the Saturday qualifying session] but the position I am in today is pretty much what I had expected. The testing at Mugello was positive but our progress can only be measured in 10ths of a second and definitely not in "a few" seconds.'

With the media hanging around waiting for a disaster and the Fiat hierarchy sitting in the background, the man right in the middle of the heat was once again Jean Todt. It was difficult to hazard a guess at what he might be thinking. However, talk to him and behind the diffident air is a sensitive and highly perceptive professional. To allow the team to work with confidence he is happy to delegate responsibility to his managers and allow them to get on with things. But that doesn't mean he is unaware of what is going on. His quick mind picks up and tunes in to other people's insecurities as well as their strengths and weaknesses.

At Nurburgring, his thoughts were on the team and his future. 'It is difficult to find good people, and that is why we have been slowly building the team, until now, when we are at the point of having very good people on board. It is then difficult to get people to work together efficiently and difficult to build stability. I like to be aware of, and in control of, everything.'

The man whose job epitomizes the expression 'the buck stops here' is under relentless pressure, but he is unlikely to give it up until he has seen it through to the end and at least one World Championship.

You don't build a team, take on the double World Champion as your Number One driver, then turn your back on it and hand success on a plate to another man.

The Mugello test had been of vital importance in more than one way. Nigel Stepney takes up the story: 'At the moment we can win or lose a race on pit stops. We have to practise on the race car as each car is slightly different and there are 20 people to co-ordinate in seven seconds. After the South American races I analysed all the pit stops to see where we were making mistakes and losing time. Shell then came to our rescue by shooting an ad all day at Mugello, which required us to do endless pit stops. It was the best practice we have ever had.'

Back in England, John Barnard was wrestling with his desire for perfection and the lack of time in which to achieve it. He wanted to continue using titanium for the gearbox casing, but time constraints had forced him to relinquish his drive to push Formula One forward into the future, and develop new ideas that in the long run would prove better and more efficient. Like many new concepts the teething problems were not difficult to rectify, but it needed that elusive element, time, and time is one thing you just don't have in Formula One racing.

At the Nurburgring Schumacher proved that he is worth the $25 million that Ferrari is paying him and, after qualifying third, came second behind the Williams of Jacques Villeneuve in the race. It was an unexpected result that delighted the thousands of Schumacher fans who crowded round the podium to celebrate. Schumacher declared, 'I didn't expect to run so close to Williams. I am pleased for the mechanics and all the crew.'

Part of the reason for his determination was a phone call from his brother Ralf, who had come third in a race in Japan and challenged his brother to beat this. He promptly did! Montezemolo was ecstatic and celebrated with the team, although like everyone he tried to play down the next race at Imola. Schumacher was about to race for Ferrari in Italy, for the first time. After the result in Germany the *tifosi* were hot for more, and nothing would dampen their spirits as they prepared to make the journey to Imola.

Imola, like Monza, is a little bit different. The *tifosi* follow Ferrari to the ends of the earth, but when Formula One comes to Italy, they really push the boat out. Flags, banners and scarves litter the banks and stands around the race track, and in keeping with Italy's reputation as a Mecca of style, Antonio Ghini, director of communications, ensures that the Ferrari fan clubs use the right marque, logo and colours. 'For years millions of products were produced and sold unofficially, but now we have developed a close relationship with the fan clubs and we ensure that they have the right products at the races. The image of the exclusive Ferrari marque must be conserved and maintained.'

Such is the passion of the Italian fans that Claudio Berro had to devise an ingenious way of getting Schumacher in and out of the track. 'We had three or four plain-clothed policemen to help us, and we could use a police escort if necessary. Schumacher used to arrive at Fiorano by car, then we would transport him by helicopter to the circuit. We had a Fiat Ulysses with darkened windows to transport him from the helicopter to the track.'

Eddie Irvine got a round of applause from the media before he had even set foot in Imola for speaking in Italian at the Fiorano press conference on the Thursday before the race. This was definitely scoring points off team-mate Schumacher who, once again, was being cautious: 'Imola is a very bumpy track. Our car has problems over bumps as the aerodynamic system is not perfect. I expect problems to get the car handling right. The chances are we won't be as successful as we were at Nurburgring. We need time to translate the changes we've made in the wind tunnel to the car. The car has potential.'

Schumacher also paid tribute to Ferrari designer, John

Barnard: 'I think Barnard is very good. The success we had at Benetton is due to a certain extent to him, as he started the car.' (Barnard worked at Benetton for 18 months until the end of 1991.) This was another example of how Schumacher protects his colleagues who are in the firing line. His ability quickly to paste over any cracks in team loyalty was going to prove vital in the months to come.

There is a great family tradition in Italy and it spreads to every aspect of the Italian lifestyle. In Italy the football teams always spend the night before a match together, to build team spirit. The Ferrari team does the same. The night before everyone left for Imola, the drivers and management had dinner with Montezemolo, who impressed calm and optimism on them in equal quantities. By this stage Jean Todt had decided that the car would not be rebuilt, but that they would work on improving the aerodynamics. He said that there should be improvements by mid-season.

One of the improvements was seen a little before mid-season. The V10 engine had been consistent and good, but there was a new improved version due at Imola which proved to be reliable, although the top speed was still a little way off its competitors. However, doubts were pushed aside as Schumacher took his first pole position for Ferrari at Imola. He pushed Damon Hill off the number one spot in the closing moments of the session, before spinning to a halt with a broken left rear track rod as he turned into the Tamburello corner.

Jean Todt was very happy with the pole position. 'This result has come from hard work and a combination of the improved aerodynamics, a more drivable engine and, of course, the power of Michael Schumacher.'

Giorgio Ascanelli was worried about the brakes rather than the engine. It had been decided that the new version of the brakes would not be run in the race, due to caution rather than any actual problem. After the second practice Ascanelli, wiping sweat from his furrowed brow said, 'I'm not happy with the way things are going. I'm not worried about the race, but I am worried that the brakes won't last the race.' It was an observation borne out from long experience. Schumacher crossed the line in second place and his car ground to a halt as the brakes gave out.

Eddie Irvine finished fourth and for the first time both drivers were in the points. Things were looking up, although new modifications were still needed, not least with the clutch which was not proving reliable and led to the difficult starts that both drivers were experiencing.

None the less, Schumacher's success entranced the Italian population. Over 10 million people watched the Grand Prix on television in Italy. That was a 55 per cent share of viewing figures and an absolute record for Formula One. There had been nothing like it since eight million people had watched Alain Prost when he drove for Ferrari in the Italian Grand Prix. It showed that people were once again believing in the prancing horse.

TIME TO PARTY?
THE MOOD WAS BUOYANT AND OPTIMISTIC

After Imola, the mood was buoyant and optimistic as the team set out for Monaco. Monaco is less about motor racing and more about parties. The motorhomes gather round the port area like colourful Lego kits at a children's party. The big boats anchor out in the bay and the rich kids go to play in a big way.

Monaco may be a party town, but during a Grand Prix

weekend it is impossible to escape the racing. Wherever you stand, the roar of the Formula One engines can be heard, and like Spa or Monza, but for different reasons, it is the one place where drivers want to win more than anywhere else. Ferrari, at least on paper, should have been in with a chance.

Schumacher's race engineer, Ignazio Lunetta, was in an upbeat mood. The race engineer is the man closest to the driver. He cares only about helping his guy to win, even against his team-mate. It is a close and trusting relationship as the race engineer is the man who translates what the driver says into changes on the car. The quiet, unassuming Lunetta had worked with Jean Alesi before Michael Schumacher arrived at Ferrari, and he was finding Schumacher a very different cup of tea.

'Schumacher is more in one line, he pushes a lot and he works very hard. Alesi was lazier whereas Schumacher is constantly stimulating work. The biggest problem is to get to know Schumacher. It is very important that I can read his thoughts and get to know exactly how he likes the car in various situations. At the moment I am doing the tests with him as well as the races. He understands things very quickly and works a lot, but he still needs to be guided as he is quite perplexed a lot of the time. However, I have never seen anyone as constantly quick as Schumacher.'

Like his team-mates, Lunetta was quietly confident about Monaco. 'The engine is good, the aerodynamics have improved and the car is easier to drive. One of our biggest problems is the clutch which is difficult to control. A little movement and it over-reacts and creates wheelspin.'

Back in England, John Barnard was also optimistic. 'The main thing I hope for is that Schumacher can qualify on the front somewhere and then he'll have a good chance as it's a very difficult track to pass on.' Obligingly, Schumacher qualified on pole position. He outpaced Hill by half a second, an incredible feat on the tight Monégasque circuit. However, he shot himself in the foot by waving to the crowd before the qualifying session was completely over and Gerhard Berger, who was still on a quick lap, crashed into the back of the Ferrari. Schumacher later apologized to Berger for going too slow.

Having had two dry days of practice, it poured with rain on race day. Schumacher had a poor start and, while still on the first lap, made a mistake at the right hander after the Loews hairpin, getting half-way onto the inside kerb, then pushing the car into the guard-rail. It was all over hardly before it had hardly begun.

To his eternal credit, Schumacher took the blame full on the chin. He returned to the team garage and apologized to everyone. Lunetta says, 'He came in looking like a beaten dog. He was devastated and said sorry to everyone. We forgave him. He gives such a lot, and he is only human; he has to make mistakes sometimes.'

Team Principal Jean Todt put it succinctly as he commented, 'Michael accepts errors from others, but not from himself.' Meanwhile Eddie Irvine had qualified seventh but had a disappointing race; he had been given an illegal push start by the marshals, then Mika Salo and Mika Hakkinen crashed into him, ending his race.

End of Monaco. Deep depression. It was quiet on the way home as everyone pondered what might have been, and wondered when the next good times would come along. However, there is nothing as contrary as Formula One and disaster can turn into victory in the space of a couple of weeks – and that was about to happen. Next stop was Barcelona and the drive of a lifetime.

CREATIVE ADVERTISING

Ferrari and Shell are a potent combination: power and passion allied to technical excellence. This message has been broadcast across the world with the help of some stunning advertising campaigns. One such advertisement, called 'The pit stop', features Eddie Irvine coming in for a change of tyres and refuelling, but instead of concentrating on the race, he wants to ensure he's using Shell petrol because he is collecting the company's model cars. Thirty million people collect these cars, and the two advertisements are seen by over a billion people in more than 100 countries worldwide.

ALL ABOARD FOR SPAIN
SCHUMACHER WAS IN A CLASS OF HIS OWN

To say it rains in Spain is like saying it snows in Switzerland. There is normal rain, and then there is Spanish rain which falls in torrents. King Juan Carlos turned up for the race and Schumacher took him for a spin round the track, pointing out the dangers of driving in the wet! From third position on the grid, Schumacher made a poor start (because of a temperamental clutch) and was briefly down to sixth before overtaking the hapless Hill, who's race was about to end.

Then Schumacher took on Berger and Alesi. By the 12th lap, he had left the others behind, was out in front and in a class of his own. He pulled away from the others at a rate of four seconds a lap. It was awesome to see and put Schumacher firmly up there with the all-time greats. The most recent comparison had been Senna's remarkable drive at the European Grand Prix at Donington in 1993.

Team-mate Eddie Irvine qualified sixth, but spun out of the race after one lap. It was a shame because Ferrari had clearly got the set-up and race strategy perfect and could have had a one–two finish.

Edward Asprey will never forget it as, by chance, nearly all of the Asprey hierarchy were at the race. 'It was a simply staggering drive by Schumacher, we were all stunned by the drama. We had never expected to witness such sheer talent and guts at such close quarters. It was indisputable proof of Schumacher's greatness. He just left everyone else standing. It was as though the rain didn't exist. We celebrated with a serious bottle of champagne on the way back.'

As Schumacher took the chequered flag, the Ferrari garage became the scene of a kind of rain dance as the team members celebrated their joy. For Ignazio Lunetta, there was the promise of a brand new Vespa from Ferrari Chairman, Luca di Montezemolo to celebrate the victory; for Giorgio Ascanelli there was the great satisfaction of knowing that the race strategy of two pit stops had worked to perfection.

Montezemolo was overjoyed, Todt relieved and happy. The media started to talk about World Championships. It was a good job no one could look into the future. Spain was a high that would be remembered fondly as the team's fortunes took a dive in the next two months. There were still problems to sort out; a new higher nose for the Canadian Grand Prix; a clutch that wasn't so difficult to use, and other small modifications to improve the aerodynamics.

● ● ●

On their own these were problems that could easily be sorted out, but combined they were about to become overwhelming and put the team under the kind of pressure that, in the past, had blown it apart.

CHAPTER THREE

The Summer of Discontent

'Every time I wake up I struggle because we are not winning. But the important thing is to keep on trying...'

Giorgio Ascanelli
*Ferrari Chief Engineer, talking
after the French Grand Prix*

Not even in their worst nightmares could any of the Ferrari team have imagined that the next two months would be as disastrous as they turned out to be. It all started on a fairly positive note, with the debut of the re-designed raised nose in Canada. This won the approval of both drivers. Schumacher said, 'It's worth between a tenth and two-tenths of a second, and more comfortable.' Irvine added, 'The car is more consistent between entry and exit of corners with the new nose.' There were also some aerodynamic modifications carried out at Maranello, which made the car less sensitive. After qualifying, things continued to look hopeful. Schumacher took third spot on the grid behind the two Williams with Damon Hill on pole position. Irvine qualified a highly credible fifth.

The atmosphere within the team was calm and relaxed. Everyone expected the cars to show progress, although no one was in any doubt that the win in Spain had been down to Schumacher's brilliance rather than the car. As Nigel Stepney says, 'The win in Spain doesn't reflect our true position. That was down to Schumacher. He was brilliant to watch. He overcomes a lot of problems and is in the same league as Senna. Drivers like that are few and far between.'

However, neither Ferrari driver finished the race. Stepney explains, 'We didn't look good on full tanks during the Sunday morning warm-up. There was a problem with the brake balance and the starter motor broke on Schumacher's car only 30 seconds before the grid was due to form.'

In fact, Schumacher was forced to start from the back of the grid, and even though he was up to seventh by the time of his pit stop on lap 41, his driveshaft broke as he got to the end of the pit lane, forcing his retirement from the race. Post-race analysis diagnosed clutch problems that had effectively overstressed the driveshaft.

Eddie Irvine lasted a mere two laps before an unidentified flying object hit his car and the push rod broke, forcing him to retire from the race. Stepney comments dryly, 'When Irvine's push rod went, he came into the pits smelling like a barbecue. This was due to the fact that there is a plank of wood underneath the car and this was quietly roasting!'

Ascanelli was as disappointed as anyone. 'Canada was a race to forget,' he said afterwards, the disappointment still etched on his face as he went on to say, 'Canada should have been one of our best circuits, but we had four or five silly problems which, quite frankly, were all foreseeable. We have to improve our reliability. Schumacher deserves better. However, there are only 24 hours in a day and we will keep on with the learning curve. I have to say that overall I'm happier with the car and happier in general with the team. We still lack confidence and tend to panic, which is what we did when we had the problem with Irvine's car. The most likely explanation for the broken push rod was impact with a foreign object, but we still tended to go into panic. We haven't got it together yet.'

NEVER SAY NEVERS!
THE FRENCH GP DIDN'T HAVE THE MOST AUSPICIOUS START

The French Grand Prix is held at Magny-Cours, just outside a small town called Nevers, an appropriate name for the coming weekend, which didn't have the most auspicious of starts. Giorgio Ascanelli looked as if he had been three rounds with Mike Tyson. He had in fact been washed off a rock and hit his chin and face during the recent violent floods that had hit Italy.

Ascanelli's mood matched his physical state. The pressure was on and there hadn't been time to assemble the cars before leaving for the circuit. This was something that would cost the team dearly when Irvine's front turning vanes were found to be illegal after qualifying. It was all very much a case of wait and see, caused in some part by the lateness of the car.

Effectively, Ferrari was being forced to try out various important new modifications either at tests just before the races or at the races. It was causing huge reliability problems. As Ascanelli says, 'Problems occur when you are trying to do something different and you push your luck. First you have to fix the 300 kilometre problem, then the 500 and then the 800, then the thousands. Everything is new this year and so we are bound to have teething problems.'

The good news was that John Barnard and his team had already started to design the 1997 car, and that would mean valuable extra testing time. It was difficult to be specific about what was wrong with the 1996 car, but lessons had been learnt. As John Barnard says, 'We did something with the aerodynamics that, when the car was in the wind tunnel, indicated its improved efficiency. We had a double floor area underneath the forward part of the side pod. The aerodynamics maps, which measure how sensitive the car is, appeared to be very similar to the 1995 car, which was driveable and comfortable. But on the track it gave the symptoms of being much more sensitive. The floor gave us aerodynamic problems which I am not going to go into, as it is useful information that we found out the hard way.

'By the time you discover this type of problem during the season, you are already behind. Naturally you try and fix the problem, which means forward development is difficult. Add to that the pressure of being a part of Ferrari and if you don't stay cool things can get out of hand.'

Eddie Irvine, as is his wont, managed to produce a few

lighter moments. The Friday Five at Five press conference, when the gathered media are unleashed on five nominated team members, was a little less 'dry' than normal. The big discussion was whether nose plasters, as seen on rugby and football players, improved breathing. It was suggested that they could be useful in motor racing. Olivier Panis, winner of the Monaco Grand Prix, confessed to having tried them and found they did improve his breathing if not his speed, at which point Irvine turned towards him and said with understatement, 'But they just make you look like a dick.'

Things turned serious when qualifying for the French GP got underway on the Saturday. It was an electrifying session; Schumacher claimed pole position after Hill, with only a few minutes left, tried to claim it for himself. He was faster than Schumacher over the first two sectors of the track, but lost time during the last third. The German domination of Europe was complete when its national football team reached the finals of Euro 96. Schumacher joked, 'We have quite a few injuries, I may have to step in.' His parting shot was that the new clutch (German, of course) on the car was proving to be reliable and efficient.

Irvine lost his sense of humour when the front turning vanes on his car were proved to be illegal after a complaint from a rival team member to Charlie Whiting, who investigated the complaint and upheld it. Schumacher's car was passed. But just how do you spot a 15 millimetre difference in a racing car in the space of a few seconds? And how did it happen?

Although this turning vane was a Maranello development, John Barnard had his own theory on the first question. 'I suspect that there was a picture somewhere in a magazine which had a front shot of the car. There are always set pieces on a racing car which act as reference points. You know the width across the front wheels, the size of the front tyres and so on, so you can very quickly scale up the other parts of the car. If you look at enough Formula One cars you tend to know where everything finishes. If something looks high you tend to get a rule out and start measuring it and you scale it and then you say, "I think that front turning vane is illegal." The next stop is to go to Charlie Whiting and ask him to check it. If it is outside the legal limit, you're in trouble and that is what happened.'

Ascanelli was his usual blunt self concerning the second question. 'The fact is that before going to France, the car was never put together at Maranello, it was put together in France and it was never checked. It shouldn't have happened, there were many mistakes from many points of view and you pay for it on the circuit. In 12 years of motor racing, I've faced many legality problems and this wasn't the worst, but it still shouldn't have happened.'

On race day, there was the unusual event of having a Ferrari on pole position and a Ferrari last on the grid, due to Irvine's disqualification for the illegal turning vane. That wasn't to last long. On the warm-up lap, Schumacher's engine blew up in a puff of smoke and his race was over before it had even begun. He didn't even have time to pull over before the Italian media picked up their poisoned pens and went to town. It was a black day for the Italian racing giants. Schumacher climbed out of the car with a thunderous expression on his face. He later admitted, 'When I got out of the car, I was so angry I could have hit someone.'

To make matters worse for Ferrari, Irvine dropped out after five laps with gearbox problems. The Italian paper *La Gazzetta dello Sport* called the French Grand Prix a funeral procession, rather than a race. True to form the media soon started to call for heads to roll, and at the top of their list was Jean Todt.

However, unlike in the past Ferrari was determined to keep its problems in house and not make public sacrifices. Ferrari Chairman Luca di Montezemolo was hot on the phone to Todt as soon as the Ferraris were out of the race. He was bitterly disappointed, but reconfirmed his faith in Todt and the team. They would sort out their problems by working hard and sticking together.

Back at Maranello, the inquest started. It was found that the engine problem was caused by incorrectly machined piston heads. Of course, it wasn't to be found only on that engine and the mechanics had to work day and night to check all the other engines. There is an inspection department at Maranello which makes spot checks on all items. It would be impossible to check every single part and would require at least 40 people working full time. This would cost a fortune and would be impractical. The pressures in Formula One mean that things can and do go wrong. The problem was that things were going wrong in a fairly catastrophic manner.

Ascanelli was as pragmatic as ever. 'Every time I wake up I struggle because we are not winning. But the important thing is to keep on trying. I believe that if we concentrate on doing the best job and don't worry about the pressure, sooner or later we will win. Personally, I'd like to achieve it sooner!'

A VISIT FROM THE BOSS
THE TENSION WAS ALMOST TANGIBLE

The pressure was on. The legendary Fiat boss Gianni Agnelli was due to visit the team at the British Grand Prix, as was Luca di Montezemolo. There was no room for mistakes. Being placed under this kind of pressure would be enough to make even the most experienced mechanic nervous. After all, Agnelli is one of the most influential men in Italy, far more important than the transitory prime ministers who come and go at regular intervals. And Montezemolo is his man and their chief.

It is in this type of situation that Schumacher comes into his own. His focused, Teutonic nature allows no interruptions during Grand Prix weekends. He refuses to do any interviews outside of the official FIA interviews which take place at pre-arranged times over the race weekend. He undertakes only minimal sponsorship activities such as brief appearances for Shell and Asprey to meet their guests. His attitude is that he is paid to race and win, and his energy must be concentrated on this task.

To this end he does not allow disturbances in the garage, and that includes the presence of bosses. If he thinks Agnelli or Montezemolo are making people nervous he will ask them to leave. Exuding the determination and confidence of a double World Champion, no one questions him. As John Barnard has said, 'Schumacher's ability to impose calm on the team has been vital.' Never more so than at Silverstone.

The team stayed at The Saracen's Head hotel in Towcester, which has been team headquarters for a number of years. The only problem is that it overlooks the road. Schumacher was not impressed. He arrived at the reception desk to complain about the noise. The receptionists were equally unimpressed by the double and current World Champion. They had regular guests who had already booked in to quieter parts of the hotel. A stand off situation was reached, which was only relieved when the Italians (as ever) found a compromise and moved another couple of people around to allow Schumacher to have a quiet room in which he could sleep.

It was at Silverstone that Edward Asprey realized what it meant to be part of the most glamorous, adored team in

Formula One. 'I was walking through the gates to the paddock, when a young boy came up and thrust his autograph book at me, along with a picture of Ferrari for me to sign. I was taken aback and said, "But I'm not part of the actual team." He just said, "But you're part of Ferrari", and I realized what it meant to be part of the mystique, power and image that is Ferrari.'

At 10.50 am on the Friday morning, Montezemolo walked into the Ferrari garage and greeted everyone. At 11.10 am, 10 minutes into the practice session, Claudio Berro and Giorgio Ascanelli took their places on the pit wall. There was still no sign of Gianni Agnelli, who was having trouble getting through security! Bernie Ecclestone and co. introduced a new system for the 1996 season, which involved everyone with pit and paddock passes going through a machine turnstile, into which they would swipe special cards, like credit cards, which recorded their arrival and departure. It was designed, with valid reasons, to stop people from handing passes through the fence once they had got into the paddock. But it was having an off day.

Eventually, Agnelli was allowed through and he walked onto the pit wall at 11.20 am with his VIP party. Todt remained in place studying the monitor in front of him. The tension in the air was almost tangible. Agnelli is rather like an agnostic Pope, in that he has absolute power. This is demonstrated by his ability to manipulate and achieve his will through quiet manoeuvres, rather than the usual Latin way of noisy, overt demonstrations of police escorts and loud exclamations. A presence such as his is rare to see. Even the normally, contentious media are respectful and quiet, and uncritical.

After his few, succinct words, he duly faded into the mists, leaving Montezemolo to take over. Montezemolo ate with the team on Friday evening and stayed until after the qualifying session on Saturday. He was also determined to impose calm and order on the team. Despite the problems, everyone was looking to the future and Schumacher was a key element. 'We are extremely pleased with Michael Schumacher and it is important to know that he is pleased with Ferrari. I've told Todt to start to talk to him about renewing his contract. I like the idea of having Schumacher for three years.' In the end Schumacher signed a four-year contract up to and including 1999.

At Silverstone Schumacher qualified third behind the two Williams cars. But there was more than a one-second gap between Williams and Ferrari. Schumacher explained that he had tested various new parts – a gearbox and suspension – at Monza and worked on improving the aerodynamics, all of which had promising results. However, as Ross Brawn was later to remark, 'Change for change's sake is not good for team progress.' The most important thing is to make a change because you are absolutely 100 per cent sure it is an improvement.

Jean Todt was less than happy. Under pressure from the media he exclaimed, 'I feel like I'm on trial in a court.' It wasn't an exaggeration. The media love scapegoats, and Todt and Barnard were in the front line – although both men remained supportive of each other and refused to attribute any blame for the team's misfortunes on one person. Todt declared, 'We are part of a team, it's our fault as a team, not one person's fault.'

After saying that the French Grand Prix was the blackest day of his life, Todt could not have imagined that things would get worse. They did.

Schumacher lasted three laps before suffering mechanical failure from a dry brake fitting. Irvine lasted only another two laps before he was forced to retire with a broken differential bearing. Schumacher was bemused rather than angry. 'We did a race distance in the last two tests, running reliably on Friday and Saturday. And then we do just three laps today. There is just no logic to it at all.'

There were cries of sabotage and foul play. However, the truth was somewhat different. A combination of the pain of evolution as the team struggled to bring consistency to a car that was not only late but also completely new, plus the dregs of problems that had begun in the past and not been completely resolved by the old guard, was to blame.

The technical debriefing meeting at Maranello the day after the Silverstone race was tense and lasted over three hours. Montezemolo needed to get to the bottom of the problems and one of his innovations was to make all the technicians responsible for their own jobs. This included sending a weekly report to Jean Todt giving details of what they had done and what they intended to do.

John Barnard was at the meeting and had come to his own conclusions. 'Irvine's differential bearing failure was a modification that hadn't been done, as it wasn't expected that this type of differential would be used again. We discussed ways to solve the problem as there was a titanium-steel bearing on the differential support which needed changing. It wasn't done and so when the original differential turned up in a race, it caused a problem.

'Schumacher's hydraulic fitting was not tightened properly at Silverstone. There is no answer to this. It must have come loose in some way. It was something that had been run many times before and had never given us any problems. You simply have no answer to things like that.

'In France, Irvine's car had the wrong valve fitted. Due to

the vibration problem there had been a problem with the gearbox moog valves. There was another valve which was of a special variety with specially strengthened parts inside to make it resistant to vibration. Apparently this wasn't fitted; instead the standard valve was fitted. The control went on the gearbox and it was history.'

'After Silverstone, the general feeling was, "How far down can we go?" and the general response was, "We can't go any further". Well, of course you can; you can fall out of the next race. The big thing after Silverstone was the total incomprehension about the loose hydraulic fitting on Schumacher's car. Everyone who worked on it – from the guy at the factory who put it together to the gearbox mechanics at the track – insisted it had been tight. What can you do? It remains a mystery.'

The problems with the gearboxes were now reaching a crescendo. As John Barnard said at the time, 'It seems that our problems had their roots in the era of the change from linear to metric measurements. Before the metric system was adopted, we used to buy our nuts, bolts and washers from the United States. They are very well organized in the States. There are books of selections of nuts, bolts, washers etc. which all adhere to NAS [National Aerospace Standard]. They are all designed from the highest grade of material available and easily accessible. As things went metric the British teams sorted themselves out with similar spec stuff, and everyone goes to the same places for high quality bolts, nuts etc. But this hasn't happened at Ferrari.

'Gradually, we had more problems with gearboxes cracking and studs cracking and so a lengthy investigation has been going on and it has revealed that the nuts have not been tightened correctly by using the prescribed torque settings.

One of the reasons for this was that if you used the correct torque setting it squashed the washer out, as the washer was cheap and soft. The question is why use cheap washers? This is something that obviously pre-dates this new era, and probably occurred because no one said you can't go round the corner to the local hardware store and buy cheap washers. I don't know. Who knows? It is so basic that it is something you really don't question. We only discovered this when David Teletti, the stress guy at Maranello, started an overall investigation when we had a lot of stud failures. We now use the correct aircraft quality washers. It was just a basic mistake that had been overlooked for years. You can't lay the blame on anyone in particular. It is just so basic that it must have been missed.'

The pressure from the media was becoming intolerable. Everyone was writing about what they *thought* was happening and very few about what was *really* happening. The man who had to act as the buffer between Ferrari and the outside world was Ferrari press chief, Giancarlo Baccini.

When he became part of Ferrari, Baccini found that the reality was different from the legend. 'I always believed what I read about Ferrari, but some journalists write what they want to write without verifying the information. This false information has never created a reaction from inside Ferrari. It was much more serene than I imagined and I discovered that there were more politics in newspapers than at Ferrari. People create stories around legends and many people had created this myth of skulduggery at Ferrari that wasn't true. It is my job to make sure that people are informed correctly, and to try and prevent false things being written. This has been a difficult period, but the most important thing is that the team has remained united.'

FEELING THE FRUSTRATION
HOCKENHEIM WAS ANOTHER RACE TO FORGET

The world held its breath at Hockenheim for the 1996 German Grand Prix, Schumacher's home race. Boris Becker turned up to lend his support to his fellow national, and Schumacher finished the race, even if it was a poor fourth. Irvine disappeared with a broken gearbox – yet another one. Montezemolo was relieved rather than pleased that at least Schumacher had finished the race. 'We wanted to finish the race and we did. Before the end of the season we count on winning at least one more race.' In the circumstances it was a brave statement. He is used to stress, but the intense pressure of the problems was beginning to get to even him.

The next race in Hungary produced more gearbox problems for Irvine, which resulted in an increase in the temperature of the oil in the gearbox so the team radioed him to stop. Schumacher had electronic problems which affected the accelerator and meant he had to switch the engine on and off on the steering wheel to go through the slow corners. Eventually it refused to fire up again and he, too, had to retire. It was another race to forget...

Irvine was frustrated but not as much as Barnard who was fuming back in England. 'I fully admit that this year's car is not as we wanted; it is not as good as I expected due to problems with the aerodynamics. I'm not covering any of that up, but we have worked to put that right. We have worked around the front wing and made a new diffuser. When I did the gearbox layout, I had in mind to do a new rear suspension and we did that. FDD did the suspension, Maranello did the diffuser. However, I informed the gearbox people at the beginning of the year that I didn't think there was enough oil flow and I thought we had a gearbox cooling problem. This went on and on until eventually they found the pressure release valve was on the wrong setting, and had been for about three years.

'At least we have discovered the problem, and it wasn't down to bad checking, but probably the wrong specification was requested at the beginning. What I find frustrating is that you bang your head against a brick wall, saying "check this, check that", and nothing happens until the gearbox has blown up in three races and eventually someone has to go and look at it and find out what is wrong. Then when you ask why it wasn't investigated, they say it is because the car is late. No one's going to go back to Schumacher and say the pressure release valve in the gearbox is at the wrong setting. No one's going to go back and say the teeth on the oil pump drive gear were incorrectly made and had an interference fit on the teeth rather than a clearance fit. The simple thing is to blame me back in England.'

So why didn't Barnard just sit down with Schumacher and tell him? 'If I sit down and tell him now, it sounds like sour grapes.'

Barnard's original agreement with Montezemolo was that he would be left alone to work in England, and so Barnard couldn't be expected to run Maranello when that had never been part of his deal. It was becoming increasingly obvious that a day-to-day hands-on technical director was needed, and needed fast. Montezemolo recognized this as a weakness and Todt was already on the case.

It can hardly be fun for the current World Champion to have to suffer the indignities of having a car that sometimes seems reluctant to get off the starting grid, let alone finish a race. Yet in times of trouble Schumacher has handled the situation with a maturity that is rare in a man who was then 27 years old.

There have been many instances when things could easily have got out of hand, but Schumacher has always kept the lid on the pressure cooker. When the press screamed for Todt's head, he coolly announced, 'Todt is the best thing for Ferrari. To get rid of him would be the worst thing Ferrari could do.' He has defended, protected and, as Nigel Stepney said, 'given shit behind closed doors'.

As the team left for Spa, it seemed as if success was as elusive as ever. Apart from the win in Spain, which was mainly due to Schumacher's brilliance rather than an improvement in the car, there were very few indications that the team was on the right track in the developments and changes it had made. However, the team dynamics had changed; it was more together and more focused. Jean Todt had succeeded where others had failed, and imposed structure and organization. Giorgio Ascanelli had kept his battalion of men working in one direction, and the hard work carried out over many days and nights was about to pay off.

● ● ●

Success and the tangible proof that the pain of the summer experience had been turned into positive progress were just around the corner.

CHAPTER FOUR

The Road to Victory

'Spa was the best win of the season.

It was like a breath of fresh air after

all the problems.'

Jean Todt
Ferrari Team Director

There was an air of depression hanging over Maranello, home of the Ferrari team. The season was nearly two-thirds over and there was just the superb win in Spain to show for it — a win that had been down to Schumacher's outstanding talent rather than any improvement with the car. Next up was Spa-Francorchamps in Belgium — one of the great circuits and a favourite with the drivers. Difficult and demanding with the awesome Eau Rouge corner to conquer, there is nothing quite like the sight of the sweeping, misty track to excite the senses of a Formula One driver. Nineteen-ninety six was no different. Spa holds mainly good memories for Schumacher. He made his Formula One debut here for Jordan in 1991 and won the race in 1992. In 1994 he won the Belgium Grand Prix again, only to be disqualified.

After an awful summer, Ferrari was in desperate need of victory. Jean Todt had suffered intolerable pressure both externally from the press and internally as the man at the top holding the ultimate responsibility. The saying 'it's tough at the top' is never truer than at Ferrari, where there is a constant change in attitude and feelings towards people. These changes may be so slight as to be hardly perceptible, but you ignore them at your peril, for combined they constitute the political current of who is in and who is out. And against a background of change and the growing pains of leading a new era, it has to be said that Jean Todt performed miracles.

THE TIDE TURNS
JEAN TODT'S SMILING FACE SAID IT ALL

Spa was a watershed. Todt arrived in Belgium with his energy levels low, and prepared once more to go into the breach and fight to the end. It was to be a weekend he would remember for a long time. Despite the poor results, he had kept team morale up and ensured that it was a united, proud outfit that arrived in Belgium to compete in the 13th round of the 1996 FIA Formula One World Championship.

The team worked well; Schumacher qualified third and looked good for a podium finish, although the same was said at Monaco and France. But this time the tide was turning. In the race itself, Schumacher slipped into second place behind Villeneuve, after Hill had made a poor start. Having managed a timely pit stop when the pace car came out after Jos Verstappen crashed, Schumacher overtook Villeneuve a few laps later and destiny decreed that the World Champion would go on to win the race, his second as a Ferrari driver. Jean Todt's smiling face said it all. The relief was enormous. Later he admitted, 'Spa was the best win of the season. It was like a breath of fresh air after all the problems.'

After the race, an inspection of Schumacher's car revealed that the gearbox casing was cracked. Although highly delighted by the win, John Barnard was once again anxious about the treatment of his 'baby'. 'The car was hitting the ground so hard at both ends that it completely cracked the gearbox cases. Even the bearings on the starter shafts were broken, and they don't do anything except when you start the car. When I was watching the race on television I noticed that our car was the only one sparking heavily off the ground. It was the set-up again.'

A top designer cannot be neutral about his creation, and it was swiftly becoming apparent that it was not only the gearbox casing that was breaking but the entire relationship between Barnard and Ferrari, poisoned by acrimonious disputes between Ferrari Design and Development (FDD) in England and the technical team at Maranello.

Barnard was convinced that things were not as they should be. He thought that certain people at Maranello were determined to use FDD and Jean Todt as scapegoats. It was too easy to say the gearbox broke again, without giving an explanation.

Giorgio Ascanelli, the man in charge of set-up, had other ideas about the cracked gearbox. 'We believe the cracking on the gearbox was due to the type of circuit that Spa is. In reality we had problems with the titanium casing cracking in Melbourne, and so had to test with the old gearbox until the middle of June, and our pattern of reliability with the new gearbox has never been constant.'

To compound the problems, when Barnard visited Maranello on 6 August 1997, Montezemolo informed him that he wanted to bring the aerodynamic development back to Italy and he wanted the FDD team to move to Maranello. It was the only way forward.

As well as affecting next year's car, this announcement effectively made Barnard's contract null and void. However, from Ferrari's point of view they were finding that it was increasingly difficult to design a car long distance via phone and fax, and although it was clear that they, and especially Jean Todt, had great respect for Barnard and his team at FDD, they also needed to have the main design centre at Maranello. It would be Barnard's decision. Ferrari would be happy to have him and his team in Italy, if not they would have to look elsewhere.

After Spa, the team was on a high again, although the next race was Monza where the pressure on Ferrari to win is unbearable. It had been eight years since Ferrari had a victory at Monza, shortly after the death of Enzo Ferrari. Now the fans demanded the ultimate, a Ferrari victory on home ground.

Against this background of expectation, the new car for 1997 was taking shape and Michael Schumacher travelled to FDD in England for a cockpit fitting with Ignazio Lunetta, his trusty race engineer, by his side.

John Barnard and his assistant Mike Coughlan were there to greet Schumacher, who was then taken into a special room and shown a mock-up of the cockpit, built to projected dimensions. There it stood in the middle of the room, like a young supermodel parading on the catwalk. And like a supermodel it had a super price. The cost of making the mock-up was estimated at about £50,000 – for that price you could buy a smart road car that has the added advantage of having an engine.

Schumacher eased himself into the car and wiggled about, and was as focused on this task as he is with everything. He commented that he had restricted vision and so the sides were shaped, although they can't be shaped too much as that would result in loss of torsion and stiffness. He wanted the cockpit lower, which would mean lowering the whole car by about 10 millimetres. He also thought the steering wheel was too high. However, lowering the steering wheel would put into jeopardy the rule that says the driver must be able to get out of his car within five seconds.

The whole day went ahead in fits and starts, things were lowered, raised, swapped, changed, Schumacher's helmet was compared to Berger's and the clearance on the air flow inlet was checked. Barnard peered at intermittent intervals into the car and listened to Schumacher intently, while also maintaining his own overall view of the situation. Both men were intent on getting it right and both had the same objective of achieving as near perfection as possible.

Bits were sheared off the side of the steering wheel,

before Schumacher pointed out that the dummy gear paddles (located on the steering wheel) were upside down! As the clock struck 1 pm, Schumacher leapt out of the car and asked where lunch was. His body is as tuned to routine as his mind. After lunch it was back to the hard slog. Andy Willard, who works on the design of the car with John Barnard, arrived. There was even time to joke. When Schumacher asked for an even *lower* cockpit, Barnard quipped that his neck was too long, and it would be easier if he had his eyes higher, like a frog, to which some wit suggested that being French, that must have been Alain Prost's key to success.

At 3 pm the steering wheel was removed in order to check Schumacher's field of vision from the cockpit. At 3.15 pm the moulding ceremony began. It was a bit like something out of a science fiction movie; the car was covered in plastic, then a thin rubber cover was placed over the seat area. All the creases were carefully eradicated before a creamy brown liquid of polyurethane foam was poured behind rubber sheeting to make a seat mould, while Schumacher sat in the seat.

At 5 pm the moulding was still being adjusted – not enough liquid results in a moulding that is not accurate; too much and the driver gets covered with a rising block of foam and risks being drowned!

Schumacher climbed out of the car to phone his pilot and delay take-off. Calm and friendly, he signed endless postcards, posters, hats and scarves before disappearing into the night, commenting that Monza could be 'heaven or hell' depending on Ferrari's performance. Schumacher takes a lot of stick for being arrogant, but he is just professional and focused. When he does a job he gives it 100 per cent.

ON HOME GROUND
THE FANS WERE ON FIRE

Come Monza, a few days later, technical problems and the finer points of design were forgotten. Sometimes in life, there are moments that if they could be captured on canvas would be described as the perfect painting. This was one of them. Northern Italy was bathed in early autumn sunshine. Gone was the scorching heat of the summer and in its place the kind of soothing heat that gently caresses the body and the soul. Combined with this was the exquisite food, wine and welcome that only the Italians know how to produce. It had all the ingredients of a memorable weekend.

The mood among the team members was upbeat. Italian music was played in the garage as the mechanics went about their usual Thursday business, unpacking, putting the car together, starting the engine and practising pit stops. The fans were on fire. After Spa, their hot desire for a Ferrari win at Monza was almost tangible. They filled the stands and the trackside enclosures.

Giorgio Ascanelli said, 'There are seven cars that can win the race, the two Williams, the two McLarens, the two Benettons and Michael. If Hill goes out we have a good chance and this means we have made progress. At the beginning of the year we weren't in a position to compete with Williams or take advantage if they fell out of the race. Now we are nearer to Williams and our objective is to be up in front on a consistent basis.'

Nigel Stepney had a hunch that this was going to be a good one. 'We knew we were in with a chance after we had a good morning warm-up.' When Alesi came into the pits, Ferrari kept Schumacher out for another vital two laps. During this time he gained two seconds as well as two laps. Schumacher then had a great pit stop and, as Stepney says, 'Every second counts and races are now won and lost on pit stops. We had problems and I proposed moving into refuelling, with someone else taking my place on front control. A lot of people were against it, but Todt didn't have a problem with it. Now it has worked, they're all for it!'

It certainly did work. Schumacher had a brilliant pit stop and came out ahead of Alesi to take the lead. The big question now was: could he maintain it? Ferrari doctor Alessandro Biffi's face was completely drained of colour as he sat immobile watching the monitor and clutching the arms of his chair. With him were friends Daniele De Lisi and Pippo De Francesco, who were also suffering the tension. A few laps from the end nobody could watch the race, but eventually destiny played a part, and Schumacher took the chequered flag and went down in history as winning his first Italian Grand Prix as a Ferrari driver.

The explosion of relief and joy in the Ferrari garage was catching. Indeed, Ferrari's oldest fan, 88-year-old Silvio Ferri, danced with delight. Ferri has been to 210 Grands Prix since the Formula One Championship started in 1950. He is the only person who doesn't need a pass – even kings and queens need one – having been given dispensation as one of motor racing's staunchest supporters. He remembers the old days of Graham Hill and Jackie Stewart, but he has a special place in his heart for Nigel Mansell. 'The best driver, always happy and content, very strong and very much a family man.'

For Jean Todt, Giorgio Ascanelli, Nigel Stepney, Ignazio Lunetta and all the team it was a moment to savour and enjoy. Ascanelli appeared soaked in champagne, wearing a Rothmans team shirt (which he had gained in a football pitch 'swap') and grinning from ear to ear. The normally cool Schumacher could not contain himself. For him it was double delight, a win at Monza and the announcement that his wife, Corinna, was expecting their first child.

The crowd, charged high with emotion, poured onto the track in front of the podium and unfurled a gigantic banner with the prancing horse in the middle. Schumacher admitted feeling the kind of warmth and emotion he had never felt before. 'It is the best day of my life. Corinna is pregnant and I have won at Monza. I've never seen so many people and felt so much emotion. I have goose bumps all over me. It is wonderful, everyone in the team deserves it.'

Second place, Jean Alesi was gracious in defeat. He had been so near to winning in his time as a Ferrari driver, and he understood what it meant. Victory at Monza was something he wanted more than anything but he said, 'It is wonderful to be on the podium with Michael and see the fans waving flags and screaming. I am really pleased Ferrari won.'

The fans crowded round the entrance to the paddock and all thoughts of leaving were abandoned. Todt and Schumacher went off to the Rothmans motorhome, climbed on the roof and let off fireworks into the night, with the compliments of the vivacious Karl Heinz Zimmerman of Rothmans.

Finally, the time came for Jean Todt and Miodrag Kotur to drive back to Maranello. When they stopped at a service station for water, the attendants crowded round wanting to celebrate and were already looking to the future. 'When will we win the World Championship?' was the burning question. Todt just smiled and promised nothing. Today was the moment to enjoy victory; there was time tomorrow to think of work again.

The only disappointed man was Eddie Irvine who had been running a strong second before going out of the race. As

Schumacher crossed the winning line, a disconsolate mechanic from Irvine's car was quietly smoking a cigarette and leaning on the back of the motorhome. The ecstasy of victory, the pain of defeat. There was a sea of happy faces in red overalls, and a sea of disappointed faces in the same coloured overalls. Schumacher did have words of consolation for his team-mate. 'He has great success with women, so he can't have success at everything!'

The mood was ebullient but steeped in reality; it was not a time to get overexcited and start dreaming of World Championships. There was still a lot of work to be done. Monza was a great victory but Nigel Stepney, like Ascanelli, was very aware that not everything was running smoothly just yet. 'We are still very careful on every aspect of safety and security. You always have to keep on top of it, but at the moment we are paying particular attention to everything as we are on the limit.'

Giorgio Ascanelli was similarly relieved that the team had made the huge psychological jump of being mature enough to live through the bad times and come out wiser the other end. 'During the problems we had in the summer, we had to keep our spirits up and stick together. I am very happy with everyone because we remained calm. A few years ago something terminal would have happened to some people and this didn't happen. Those same people who would have been fired, were left alone to resolve the problems quietly and calmly. This is positive for everyone as it helps build team spirit and loyalty, and give people the space to sort things out without forever looking over their shoulders. The boys are together out there even when the going gets tough. Having said this I'm not saying we've fixed all the problems, but we have fixed a lot of them. We still have problems with the clutch and that is annoying us as good starts are vital. Look at Monza, we nearly compromised the victory due to Alesi's magnificent start and our poor one. But things are moving forward. We have avoided some of the old problems, we didn't break a push rod in Spa, we haven't broken a wheel bearing in Monza, all of which were old traditions of ours! We did manage to lose some bodywork in Monza on the Saturday, but apart from that we are in pretty good shape.'

Ascanelli may be the boss at the track, but he doesn't encourage star status. 'The mechanic who sets the rear tyre pressure is as important as the guy who decides race strategy. Everything is important at different levels. We work as a team and that is truer now than it has ever been.'

Despite the magnificent win at Monza and his relief, Ascanelli was also strangely subdued. 'You are never in a condition to ease off the pressure. Enzo Ferrari used to tell me that it takes a lifetime to build up fame, a good reputation and respect, and you can lose it all in a minute. No matter how good it looks, and it looks as though we are finally coming out of the tunnel, we can be back in it again in five minutes if we make a mistake.'

And that is the essence of Ferrari. Nothing is ever good enough, tomorrow is always just around the corner and if you mess things up then victory is quickly forgotten.

Spa and Monza were both hard races, and one of the most satisfying aspects of the victories was that the new V10 engine had performed well in its first year, with very few reliability problems. Apart from France, it had worked well and had already made several evolutionary steps to producing more power and improved drivability, while maintaining reliability. Paolo Martinelli is head of the engine department. A quiet, self-effacing, almost shy man, he has been working at Ferrari for 18 years and has made his way to the top, through the road car side and then within Formula One. As with most of his colleagues time is tight and the pressure is always on.

Martinelli has been quietly impressed with the V10's first year. 'We started off quite well and then made a significant improvement in terms of performance, power and drivability from Imola onwards. We managed to have better combustion and air distribution using a little more air, so we had much better efficiency. We had our first pole position at Imola and four in total, which was impressive for the first year. Schumacher is a big contributor to our success. He is very mature and never complains. He describes in detail any defect or request, modification or improvement. His input is very precise. He can describe each corner, the critical area of the revs and then together we work out what is best.

'Shell has also been vital to our progress. As well as providing an excellent service in terms of research and development, and the analysis service, it has also picked up other areas where potential problems could have occurred, by identifying metals in the lubricant after practice and after the race. This helps us to identify areas of the engine that are wearing and is vital in our search for perfection.'

The basic idea in any car is to get maximum power and efficiency in the engine with minimum wear and tear and maximum fuel efficiency. The core point is the input of air and fuel into the engine through the valves. The process of opening the valves occurs through the cams on the cam shaft. These rotate and open and close the valves. At Shell's Research Establishment at Thornton, Simon Dunning overseas the Formula One programme, and one of the more fundamental areas of research is the valve train. At the moment the cam effectively hits the valve and opens it up, in goes the air and fuel before the valve closes again, combustion takes place and energy is created which drives the engine. Now the next stage, which will vastly improve the road cars, is to have an indirect method of valve operation in the form of a finger-like contraption that will sit on the cam and actually open the valve. This will have the advantages of being lighter and allow the valve to open more quickly and, therefore, 'breathe' better. This is a real technological breakthrough and Shell's John Bell, who is internationally recognized as a leading 'valve train' expert, and Ferrari's Christoph Mary, spend hours hidden away in their respective offices, discussing and developing this piece of technology.

THE SEASON ENDS
NOW IT WAS TIME TO TAKE STOCK

In the car on the way back to Surrey from his wind tunnel facility at British Aerospace in Bristol, John Barnard spoke to Jean Todt and told him that FDD was still on target for an early January launch. Barnard also wanted a meeting with Todt to discuss his future. Barnard's contract was due to run out in July 1997 and with the length of time required to build a car, the situation needed to be clarified. He arranged to send a proposal to Todt and then meet him in Italy to discuss things further. The moment of final reckoning was drawing closer.

The last two races of the season went well. There was a heart-stopping fight for second place in the Constructors' Championship. In Portugal, Schumacher snatched third place from Jean Alesi and Eddie Irvine hung onto fifth place from Alesi's Benetton team-mate Gerhard Berger. This put

Benetton into second place ahead of Ferrari by just one point. Like the Drivers' title, the Constructors' Championship went down to the wire. In Japan, Stepney was feeling the pressure. 'The most important thing is that both of our cars finish the race and then we will beat Benetton to second place.'

That was the theory but as Stepney admits, 'The last two laps were hell. Berger was quick but he made a couple of mistakes and took Irvine out. Alesi went out which gave us some breathing space. Finally, Michael clinched it for us as he came second. For me this was one of the most important moments of the year, as it consolidated everything we had done. Coming second in the Constructor's Championship is a great achievement as it means the team is progressing and we are working along the right lines.'

The year was over, and now it was time to take stock and look to next season. The 1997 car was on schedule and due to be unveiled at the beginning of the year. That would give the team a valuable two months for testing before the first race in Australia.

Despite the caution there was a buzz about Ferrari that hadn't been there for many years. There was an underlying feeling of optimism. When the next prancing horse came out of its stable, there was a fair chance it could be first past the winning post, or at least give the competition a good run for its money.

THE WINTER BREAK
NOTHING STAYS THE SAME FOR LONG

As the winter winds descended on England, John Barnard flew to Italy (along with Vijay Kothary and Andy Smith) to sort out not only his future, but also that of his 40 employees. On arrival, he was involved in a Direction Meeting with Todt and the heads of departments, while Vijay was discussing budgets and Andy the materials side of things. Afterwards, the feeling was upbeat. Even the normally cynical Barnard was quietly pleased with the way things had gone and felt there was still a basis for a relationship between FDD and Ferrari, Italy. He had made it clear that he would not move to Italy, and so this had affected the nature of the relationship, but FDD could still be useful to Ferrari.

However, the fact that the relationship between Barnard and Ferrari had not broken down to the point of involving solicitors, was due largely to the diplomatic talents of Jean Todt. One of Todt's most important characteristics is his ability to make his workers feel secure and protected. Todt and Schumacher have formed a particularly warm relationship. 'I've found he seems different to outsiders than to how he actually is in reality. But most people think the same about me,' says Schumacher. 'They think I'm a strange person and they can't get close to me as I don't let them. Well, I can't let everyone get close to me and its difficult to sort out on a race weekend who is nice and who isn't, so I just concentrate on my job and shut out the rest. But I can say that Jean Todt is one of the nicest people I've met in Formula One. He looks after me like a father. There are very few people in business like him, it gives you faith in the human race.'

Michael Schumacher has few pretensions about life. Put him in the countryside with his dogs and a packet of Bonio and he is in his element. As the season ended, he took off to his house near Geneva and sought to return to being Michael Schumacher, the man, rather than Michael Schumacher, Superstar. In the company of his heavily pregnant wife, Corinna and his four dogs, he was finally able to relax for a few days. Schumacher would undoubtedly like to have more spare time, but time is short and is never wasted.

As the Ferrari team was busy preparing show cars for exhibitions and the motor shows and re-grouping for next season, Schumacher was improving his fitness. He is one of the fittest – if not *the* fittest – drivers in Formula One, but for a perfectionist that is not enough. He wanted to be in peak condition to meet the demands of the 1997 Grand Prix season. To this end, he went to Portugal for four weeks for special training with the German Olympic team. He also went to Norway for several weeks to ski with friends and to work on his fitness programme.

As Schumacher was passing through the barriers of fitness, his team-mate Eddie Irvine was following his own relaxation and fitness programme. He finally got into the car for some testing in the middle of December. He then had three days' holiday, before flying to Portugal to meet some friends for three days. He went back home for Christmas and was back on the track on 3 January.

Having Michael Schumacher as a team-mate is not easy, as Martin Brundle, Ricardo Patrese and Johnny Herbert found out. Irvine's natural 'devil-may-care-attitude', coupled with his outspoken manner, indicated that relations between the two would be fraught, but to his eternal credit, Irvine has emerged a winner off the track, if not on it. Despite a dreadful season, due in part to an almost complete lack of testing, he had, unlike some of Schumacher's previous team-mates, refrained from whinging.

'The guy [Schumacher] is brilliant. He is just unbelievable. I can see that he could have a negative effect on his co-driver. You see his times and you think, "Fuck, I've got to push really hard to do that time", when in a sense you don't. You have to sit back and let it happen and then you'll get close to him. He's a genius so if you try and match his time you get freaked out and it all goes wrong.'

SONIA IRVINE'S RACE DAY

8.10 am   Am already at circuit. Collect Eddie from helicopter pad.

8.20 am   Arrive in pit lane. Prepare Eddie's breakfast.

8.45 am   Prepare Eddie's rehydration drinks for the day.

9.00 am   Organize race clothing. Check on changes to day's events.

9.15 am   Arrange for Eddie to autograph hats, photographs etc.

9.30 am   While Eddie is out for warm-up, I prepare his carbohydrate drinks and eat my breakfast.

10.00 am   Drinks taken to drivers' briefing.

10.15 am   Eddie's guests shown around Ferrari pit.

10.45 am   More drinks taken in to Eddie, read fan mail and respond (Eddie always signs the mail himself).

11.15 am   Escort Eddie to PR event.

11.30 am   Prepare post-race food.

12.00 pm   Check venue for 12.15 PR event.

12.15 pm   Collect Eddie from technical meeting and take him to the event.

12.20 pm   Prepare physio room for Eddie's massage.

12.40 pm   Eddie's massage.

1.25 pm   More drinks and final photo session organized. Hat, umbrella and drinks bottle taken to starting grid.

2.00 pm   Watch race start then return to motorhome to treat two people during the race.

5.00 pm   Take Eddie to helicopter pad. Return to pits.

5.30 pm   Drinks bottles collected and washed. Physiotherapy equipment packed away. Collect all pit passes.

6.00 pm   Eat my lunch!

Eddie's sister Sonia is an important part of 'Team Irvine', as are his delightful parents, Edmund Senior and Kathleen. A qualified physiotherapist, Sonia travels with her brother as his physio, but more than that she is also his organizer. 'Sonia is a great organizer,' says Irvine. 'I need her as much to organize me as for my physio.'

Sonia is enjoying the job, which is demanding and involves everything from keeping Eddie's muscles loose to making sure he attends his sponsors' functions on time and at the right place. But it is also an extension of their big sister/little brother relationship. Unlike Michael Schumacher who has been known to keep his physio/personal trainer Balbir Singh up past midnight when he wants a massage, Eddie is an early bird. As Sonia says, 'Although his room is still a mess, like it was when we lived at home, he loves his bed. He's in it by 10 o'clock, which means I can also have an early night, or join the rest of the team for a nightcap, depending on whether I'm tired or not.' A slim, attractive blonde with a very open, pleasant personality, Sonia is ultra fit herself and does regular one-hour runs before working out in the gym for a further couple of hours.

One of the reasons for Irvine's early nights could be his almost pathological hatred of the trappings of fame. Having a famous face is one thing he hates, and although he is no newcomer to Formula One racing, he has discovered that being a Ferrari driver is different to being behind the wheel of a Jordan car. 'I really don't like people gawping at me. I like to get up, throw on some clothes and a pair of trainers, and wander down to breakfast in the hotel. Now people stare at me. They may be saying, "Look at that messy bastard", but if I wasn't famous, they wouldn't be staring in the first place. It's much worse being a Ferrari driver than it was when I was at Jordan. If I do anything I hear it back totally different, with piles of top-spin on it. From raking the garden, it changes to me having a fight with my neighbour.'

● ● ●

As the year came to a close, Jean Todt was in a reflective mood. It had been a hard season, his head had been on the line more than once, but there had been some good moments like Spain, Spa and Monza. But were they enough to make up for the pain? 'I've no time to be happy, I have to work,' says Todt.

Three wins had been the objective for 1996, and that had been achieved but Todt was not happy. 'Officially, we achieved our objectives, but deep down I think we could have done better. We had a lot of problems, but at the end of the day it all worked quite well.'

The end of the year is a time to let the imagination run a little wild after the pent-up pressures of racing. Jean Todt is happy when he is back in France with his family including his son Nicholas. Those precious moments spent with family and friends are what recharge his batteries. At Maranello, 'in the middle of nowhere' as he puts it, there is no escape. 'I work a 15-hour day; everyone thinks it's fantastic as I'm travelling all the time, but I don't actually get to see anywhere.'

When he leaves the office, the cool professional becomes a man driven by his heart. At the end of 1996 he announced that he had fallen in love with a young woman whom he had met through Flavio Briatore. 'My heart is behind my private life, but in my professional life it is different, you don't belong to yourself, you have to think of others and the right way to go.'

A round of Christmas parties completed the 1996 season. Shell had a party in London on December 1996 high up in the

Shell Centre overlooking the River Thames near Waterloo. The ever-enthusiastic and well-informed Roger Lindsay (who had been at the front of the oil company's involvement with Formula One since the beginning) was already upbeat about 1997. 'I'll eat my hat if Schumacher doesn't win the World Championship,' he declared.

On the 21 December there were two more parties – one at Ferrari Headquarters in Italy, held at lunch time, and one at Ferrari UK in England. Some employees, such as John Barnard and Jean Todt, attended both by shuttling from one to the other in a private jet. The mood was generally upbeat and at the Ferrari UK party, Jean Todt promised the FDD employees that talks were going on to resolve the contractual situation between Ferrari and FDD. The reality of it was that Barnard wouldn't remain as chief designer as Todt wanted everything under one roof, but there was a general feeling that specialist parts and innovative projects for the future could still remain with FDD.

● ● ●

However, as the New Year dawned it would soon become apparent that nothing stays the same for long, particularly in the high octane world of Formula One motor racing.

CHAPTER FIVE

New Beginnings

'I don't want to be treated as special because I'm not. I just drive a racing car round in circles a bit faster than anyone else.'

Michael Schumacher
on his position within the team

It's 7 January 1997. Jean Todt, John Barnard and engine man Paolo Martinelli line up on the stage to face the world's press like three prisoners facing the firing squad. The ever capable, unflappable Bob Constanduros was the host, co-ordinating questions and live television links. On the stage stood the new car, the Ferrari F310B, shrouded in red silk, awaiting the moment when she would be unveiled to the world.

Jean Todt started the proceedings and was clearly pleased to have the car completed earlier than last year. 'It's very important to have the car six weeks before the first race, so we can do the tests we want to do before the start of the 1997 season.'

The problems encountered with the car just prior to the beginning of the 1996 season had been almost disastrous. (To begin with, the car was very late in being completed, then there were endless logistical problems surrounding the car being tested, and finally, at the first race of the season, the team encountered an unexpected problem with the gearbox casing. The only bright spot on the horizon had been Eddie Irvine's third place in that opening race in Australia.) Todt didn't want a repeat performance. He is not a naturally ebullient man and exuded a quiet confidence rather than outright optimism. Michael Schumacher was also playing it down. He was keen to point out that '1997 will be a direction year in which we aim to build for the future. Our aim is to improve over last year in terms of reliability and success.'

Luca di Montezemolo, the energetic Ferrari chairman, took to centre stage for the unveiling, and to a reverent silence the shrouds were removed to reveal a car that was somewhat similar to a Williams or a Benetton. It was a high-nosed, conventional car that, most importantly, was ready a full two months before the season began.

Montezemolo was also playing things down. He wanted 'to win more races than last year, but we must keep our feet on the ground'. However, there was an optimism that hadn't been apparent in 1996; the team was more united and clearer in its direction. Schumacher had been with Ferrari for a year, and his influence was already strong. It was no surprise when ex-Benetton technical director, Ross Brawn, switched allegiance. Technical co-ordination was something that Ferrari needed badly, particularly after some of the problems of 1996.

Brawn had spent four-and-a-half years with Schumacher at Benetton. It was a highly successful partnership, culminating in two World Championships in 1994 and 1995. Although he wasn't in the firing line on the stage, Brawn was in the background and was besieged by the media once the official presentation was over and the scramble for interviews began. He is, however, by nature a very calm and collected character. A veritable gentle giant in a sea of hysteria.

The presentation of the new car was a baptism of fire for him; the main question was how would his arrival affect John Barnard's position within Ferrari? Although officially John Barnard was the chief designer, which meant that Brawn as technical director was not a threat, the truth of the matter was that negotiations were pretty far advanced for Barnard to purchase Ferrari Design and Development (FDD) and run it as his own company. He would still maintain contact with Ferrari and make specialist parts, but Ferrari design and development would return to Maranello. It was difficult to keep the lid on the pan and deflect questions, but it was achieved by Jean Todt's declaration that talks between Ferrari and Barnard had just started.

THE 1997 SEASON
PEOPLE WERE BEGINNING TO SMELL ANOTHER WORLD CHAMPIONSHIP

On the 8 January, Barnard and Todt met at Maranello with lawyers to try and make progress, although it was to be another month before an agreement was actually reached. It was decided that FDD would become B3 Technologies; Barnard would eventually join Arrows, as would quite a few of his employees, but the core of the company would remain at Shalford. More streamlined, with 30 employees, Barnard's new organization would still have the capacity to produce high-quality, innovative components to continue his desire to be at the cutting edge of technology. In due course B3 would look to expand its core business into other areas of the high technology business.

Meanwhile, Schumacher's seat in the new car was still not right and it took two late nights to get it right. FDD's head of composites, Peter Brown, materialized in the reception of the Hotel Executive one morning and was taken to the factory to sort it out. He later joined Ferrari from FDD.

Despite the caution expressed by everyone at the presentation of the new car (apart from Fiat boss Cesare Romiti who gently took Ferrari Chairman Luca di Montezemolo to task for being so cautious in his predictions for 1997), behind the scenes the story was a little different. Heiner Buchinger, Schumacher's press guru and one of the people closest to the German driver, was convinced that his boy would be World Champion for a third time by the end of the 1997 season. Buchinger is an unflappable character with a keen sense of humour. However, he was deadly serious in his insistence that Ferrari would have a World Champion for the first time since Jody Scheckter won the title in 1979.

Schumacher has been in the public eye for over seven years

since bursting into Formula One, but there is no let up in the media's hunger for more and more information. Buchinger can get 30 or more calls a day from the press, all requests for one-to-one interviews, which are only allowed at test sessions, as at the races, Schumacher attends official press conferences only. Schumacher, like his team-mate Eddie Irvine, craves normality and a respite from the heavy mantles of fame. 'It's a bit easier living in Switzerland, but not as private as it used to be, and not as I would like to have it. I have certain dreams and one of them is to be treated like a normal human being who can walk around the streets like anyone else. I don't want to be treated as special because I'm not. I just drive a racing car round in circles a bit faster than anyone else.'

An ordinary man with an extraordinary talent. As the media pack were camped out in the Hotel Executive and the Hotel Domus, wonderboy was settling into Enzo Ferrari's old house, which is inside Fiorano right next to the track. The Old Man used to like to be near the cars and the engineers, so he knew what was going on. For Schumacher it is a haven of peace and gives him the opportunity to live like a normal person. On the outside it is a pretty standard two-storey house, complete with shutters, but walk inside and a sense of wonder takes over. On the ground floor near the entrance is a room with over 25 prancing horses displayed round it in varying sizes and made from various materials.

Walk up the stone steps and into the room on your left and you step back in time. The walls on all four sides are covered with black and white photographs of the glory days – Fangio, Gonzalez, Hawthorne and Surtees ... every spare inch is covered with a memory. Even the clinical Schumacher feels the history. 'There is a different feeling to Enzo Ferrari's house; it has a very special atmosphere. I feel at home there in my little apartment (a room and bathroom), where I have a television with satellite channels. If the car has a problem I can go back to the house and watch television. Also my family can come and visit me.'

Ferrari has always attracted a large following, but since Schumacher's arrival the level of interest has increased. As the owner of the Il Montana restaurant, Maurizio Paolucci, explains: 'Since Schumacher arrived, it's been like a pilgrimage here. Ferrari is very important, it's the heartbeat of Maranello.' Despite attempts by the Ferrari hierarchy to play it cool, the ordinary people on the street were beginning to smell another World Championship, and nothing was going to put them off the scent.

On the morning of the 8 January, out of the cold mists of winter, the familiar sound of the V10 engine could be heard throughout Maranello. The locals appeared on the bridge that overlooks the circuit but is not part of the private grounds. The engineers and workers gathered and so did the chairman. This was the moment when reality would take over from the previous day's hype. It was also Ross Brawn's induction into Formula One's most historic team.

The volatile Giorgio Ascanelli was directing the action. Tense and emotional, he was intent on getting it right and making sure everyone knew their responsibilities. As his commands grew louder, John Barnard smiled to himself and looked over at Ross Brawn. It was Brawn's baby now. Meanwhile, the car continued to lap the track, until after 31 laps there was a united sigh of relief. No major problems. Basically, the car was sound. Schumacher jumped out and declared: 'It feels better than last year; it feels more balanced and I think we can make progress.'

On 9 January there was a snow blizzard, so testing was suspended. Barnard was out of Maranello like a shot. He wanted to get home, back to the tranquillity of Surrey where he could think in peace without this madness going on round him. As the dark, low outlines of the Ferrari factories disappeared in a cloud of snowflakes, little did he realize that this would be his last view of the home of the prancing horse. He would not return again – at least, not as a part of the Ferrari team.

A week later Jean Todt called Barnard to say that Ferrari had appointed ex-Benetton man Rory Byrne as chief designer. It was the end of the Shalford era. Barnard says, 'Back in September 1996, Jean asked if I would move to Italy and I said "No". From this point it was obvious that we were going to go our separate ways. It was just a case of agreeing on a price for FDD. Jean went out with his shopping basket and started the search for a technical director/chief designer, and he got Ross Brawn. Even though Ross is a technical director he got most of the accolade for Benetton's success, and I think Jean thought he'd got both a technical director and a designer. But having established that Byrne was the designer he went out again and got him – and the team was complete.'

It appeared that money was no barrier to the team, a fact that Barnard confirmed. 'Before Schumacher's arrival, we were always being told to cut back on costs, cut personnel, even cut the tests. But when Schumacher joined, it was like another world had opened up.'

The source of the money is a well-kept secret, but it is likely that a good percentage came from new partners Shell, the mother company Fiat and new sponsors Asprey. However, the serious finances in 1997 seemed to come from Philip Morris who had ceased supporting McLaren and were now concentrating on Ferrari. In return for funding a large percentage of the budget, the team became Scuderia Ferrari Marlboro, and the deep red colour so long associated with the car was changed to a more electrifying tomato red.

People in the know put the total budget for 1997 in the region of £90 million with almost 50 per cent going on engine design, development and production. According to a Ferrari insider: 'At the beginning of last season we were on engine block 40; by half-way through the season we were on 130. That is a hell of a lot of engines to get through and accounts for the substantial cost of development. However, when you are designing a new engine you have to spend a lot of money. And bearing in mind the reliability of the V10, it was money well spent. No other team has put a new engine on the market and had it perform so well so consistently.'

The end of the Barnard era had left its mark. Ferrari had the latest gearbox technology, as well as uprights, bearings and hubs that are well and truly proven and as good as anything you'll find today. The basic manufacturing process was in place. Now the new boys could pick it up and rather than have to build a new car from scratch, they could concentrate on getting the shape of the car right. Even the innovative parts were well in place – for example, the titanium uprights which Ferrari had been using since 1994 and which no other team uses at present.

Barnard works to a simple philosophy and that is to make life simple for the mechanic. The torsion bar springs that he developed in 1989 are lightweight springs which are quick to change – much quicker than a conventional coil spring. He was also the first person to create the quick-lock nose box catch, which enables mechanics to change the nose box in seconds.

However, according to Barnard, the biggest problem is the press. 'Go to a test and they make a big thing out of the fact you haven't run fastest. It's always time, time, time, even when you are testing some new part where time isn't the most important aspect. The pressure from the press is enormous and very negative to actually achieving anything. Regarding the day-to-day politics at Ferrari, it is all about covering your arse and I think it was too easy for the two companies (Italy and FDD) to blame each other every time something went wrong.'

Nevertheless, Barnard has respect for Todt who he thinks 'is a decent man. I liked him ... he has a very difficult job.' But that doesn't mean there will be a third Barnard term. 'Nineteen ninety-seven was my last car for Ferrari. There will not be another.'

The sad thing is that Barnard should have been around to see the fruits of his work. Perhaps if both sides could have compromised he would still be with Ferrari, and together with the team as it is and with Ross Brawn it would have the best chance of winning the World Championship. Barnard had no need to move to Italy with Brawn in place. He just needed to keep in more regular contact and move certain parts of the empire abroad.

It had undoubtedly been a fraught five years. Barnard was disappointed not to see things through to their natural conclusion, a World Championship. 'That would have been nice, but to be honest I'm not entirely convinced Ferrari can do it now. I hope they do and I wish them well. Ferrari back at the top is good for everyone in motor racing.' But surely he must have had *some* good memories. With a devilish grin on his face he says, 'Well, that's a difficult one. It's a bit like spending five years in prison and being asked what the best moments were.'

Exit John Barnard. Or nearly. He did head out to the first test in Barcelona, where the car looked good despite several engine blow-ups. Paradoxically, it was almost the result of being too good in 1996. Having got 95 per cent right at the first go, it is very difficult to fine-tune the last 5 per cent. Engine Chief Paolo Martinelli was not unduly worried. 'We know the problem and we know how to fix it, so we will soon have reliability again.'

Meanwhile Ferrari had agreed a deal to supply engines to Sauber. With the engines went Japanese engine wizard Goto and, some suspected, the best of the step-one engine. When asked about the Ferrari engine for 1997, one team member commented that it was 'slightly less powerful, slightly less reliable and slightly heavier than the one we've sold to Sauber'.

Off the track, Schumacher became a father for the first time when his daughter Gina Maria was born on 20 February 1997. He describes it as the best moment of his life. 'The most outstanding impression of my life was holding her in my arms for the first time, especially after all the difficulties I had in getting to the birth on time. I was testing at Mugello, it was late at night and the airports were closing. I didn't want to miss it, but I was a bit frightened about what would happen in terms of whether I would feel ill [during the birth] or suffer in some way. I didn't want to let Corinna down. However, it made me the happiest man in the world. Having seen it, I never want to miss it again – however many more times it happens!'

Towards the end of the 1998 season, the Schumachers announced that they were expecting their second child. But, as Michael says, 'It's hard on Corinna as I'm travelling most of the time. If I'm not racing, I'm testing. Having a baby certainly changes your life. When we are both at home we are there 24 hours for the baby, unless Grandma takes over and gives us a break. We love it but it changes your life.'

EARLY SEASON FLYAWAYS
IT WASN'T A DISASTROUS START TO THE SEASON

Back on the track the first real test for Ferrari was the opening race of the 1997 season in Australia. Schumacher and Irvine qualified third and fifth respectively for the race in Melbourne.

It was no big surprise that the Williams duo were on pole and second place. In the race itself, Irvine went out on lap 1. He was overtaking on the first corner and took out Villeneuve, himself and Johnny Herbert. The others criticized Irvine, but he defends himself: 'Villeneuve had left the door open, he had braked too early. I got down the inside of him, so it was my corner. You don't win races – well I suppose sometimes you do – by sitting back. Sometimes you have to get stuck in.'

Schumacher picked up a valuable six points for his second place and Irvine more than made up for his hastiness in Australia by having a blinding third race of the season in Argentina, when he finished second. As he says, 'I made a great start and went from seventh to third. Was I hasty then? You have to take a chance and go for it. That's what racing is all about.' This result was his best Ferrari result to date, and it was an example of getting it right.

Ross Brawn had got his feet under the table by Argentina and also felt it was a good race. 'There was quite a lot of teamwork involved in terms of strategy, decisions on the tyres [they went for soft rubber] and so forth. I was much more involved with that than in the first race. However much testing or time you spend at the factory, going to the races is a different situation. Until you've done it, you can't judge where you want to be and where you want to go.'

For once Schumacher was not having a good time in Argentina. Having made a poor start he touched Barrichello's Stewart, which sent the German into a spin. Unlike two weeks earlier in Brazil, the race was not re-started, and the ex-World Champion was left fuming at the side of the track. The only good thing, apart from team-mate Irvine's second place, was that his brother Ralf, driving a Jordan, finished a worthy third and earned a podium place in only his third Grand Prix.

In between Australia and Argentina, Brazil had proved to be a nightmare – as ever for the Ferraris – and both drivers complained of lack of grip. Schumacher hung on for a fifth place and two points, while Irvine was experiencing his own hellish race. Forced to take the spare car, which is set up for Schumacher, he soon discovered that his team-mate's seat belts were not to his design and had to make a stop for them to be adjusted to end the agony in his private parts! None the less, he finished a gallant, if unimpressive, 16th.

The lack of grip had been due to the wrong tyres, but this was a complex decision as Giorgio Ascanelli explains. 'On the Saturday morning we chose to go for hard tyres, and in fact we were the only ones who did the same times in the morning as the afternoon. But the race was run on 22 degrees of asphalt and everyone who chose the softer tyres went well. It's very difficult as now we have to make a decision on which tyres to use for qualifying and the race before qualifying starts on the Saturday, so we can only base our decision on the weather forecast. In Brazil on race day we had an overcast sky with a warm track. This is very rare. It didn't happen during the 15 days before the race or for the 15 days after. It happened on the *day* of the race and it wasn't seen on the forecast.'

The other teams were obviously reading another weather forecast!

Between the Brazilian and Argentinian Grands Prix, the team had taken a holiday in Punta del Este in Uruguay. It was five days of relaxation and peace. Being the closed season in Uruguay, there were few people around and it was a good time to build team loyalty and spirit.

Flyaway races are complex due to their distance from the factory. If problems occur it is difficult for the team to sort them out properly until returning to Europe and using the wind tunnel for more testing. Still, it hadn't been a disastrous start to the new season.

EUROPE AGAIN
THE HEAT WAS ON

After Argentina came the first real tough test – the San Marino Grand Prix at Imola in Italy. The Italian fans are notoriously demanding and with the first race in Europe at home, it wasn't going to be easy. The man in the hot seat was Ross Brawn, and he was getting to know what it was like working for Ferrari. In the business he is known as a big man with a big heart, who issues commands with a smile even when under the greatest pressure. However, when required he can be tough and hard, and those whose work is not up to standard do not escape.

'There's a lot of pressure at Ferrari; people expect a lot,' says Brawn. 'Sometimes people expect things because its Ferrari, but in reality you have to earn everything you get. Nothing comes free.'

Brawn was pleasantly surprised by his initial findings at Ferrari. Despite the laid-back image of the Italians, he found the people enthusiastic and hard-working. The first few months were spent on a company audit. 'The assessment of what we have and how we can improve it is an ongoing situation. It's like spinning plates on top of sticks. You get them all going, then some start to wobble, and you have to go and get them going again. That's what it's like.'

The general interim report was that manufacturing was very good, and Ferrari has a very good race team. But the weak point was having to put together a design team from scratch. Brawn was also having to work with a car with which he hadn't had input from the start – and that was causing a few hold-ups.

'There are some things I'd like to do with the car that I can't do at the moment as it's been designed and conceived in a certain way. It's going to take a few more months before we see the benefit of those things. My opinion is that we need some extra improvements on the mechanical side of the car and the aerodynamics. There's a certain approach I'd like to investigate as to how we run the car in terms of its setting, but at the moment I can't. I think it was this constraint that caused our performance difficulties in Brazil. We couldn't set the car up as I and certain other team members consider to be appropriate for Brazil.'

There was a test programme of mechanical changes in force and also a weight-saving programme. Weight is another vital element in Formula One. The cars are weighed with the drivers in them. There is a minimum weight that has to be adhered to, and the idea is to get as near that weight as possible – and that doesn't mean starving the driver!

The heat was on, but Brawn was looking forward to it rather than being scared by it. 'Obviously, there's a lot of atmosphere as it's Italy. I'm looking forward to achieving some success for these people. You only have to look at Monza last year [When Schumacher won the race] to see how special it is and I'd like to experience that first hand. The only pressure is friends asking for passes!'

On the first day of practice at Imola, Irvine and Schumacher were the fastest but, as ever, Friday times mean very little. Some teams are on race set-up, some aren't, some are on full tanks and on different tyres. It drives the press mad as they never have a reference point from which to draw stories. (To try and compensate for this the FIA has introduced another press conference which is held on the Thursday afternoons of race weekends, in addition to those held on Fridays.)

However, the important session is Saturday qualifying, and that told a different story with Schumacher third on the grid and Irvine ninth. Schumacher, for once, was positively euphoric declaring, 'The gap to the Williams is not as big as in the previous races. Tomorrow I think we can get on the podium and if we get our race strategy right, then I could finish higher than my starting position.'

The fans wanted a win. Camped out on the Rivazza hill, which was a mass of red flags and banners, they expected the impossible. Being a target of their passions is not always a pleasure. Miodrag Kotur, part of the Ferrari logistics team, knows what that's like. 'Last year after our success at Monza, the fans wanted to touch anyone that was part of the Ferrari team. Well, I can tell you it's a frightening experience when 10,000 people want to touch you. It must be like being a rock star, without the minders.'

As well as being in charge of pit boards, Kotur is directly responsible for taking care of team uniform. He likens it to being in charge of an army, where every button, bootlace and belt has to be in place. It's a demanding job that rarely allows him much time at home in Paris with his wife. It also has its amusing moments, such as at the 1996 British Grand Prix. Silverstone didn't offer much joy to either of the Ferrari drivers. To cap it all, after the first practice session, the main sponsors Marlboro were waiting with faces like thunder, demanding to know why their logos were upside down on Schumacher's overalls. Miodrag recalls that he spent the rest of the afternoon with his sewing kit, unstitching the badges and replacing them the right way round!

And so, at this stage in the season Williams might have had their noses in front, but the passion was very definitely red...

APPLYING SOME PRESSURE
SCHUMACHER WANTS TO WIN

Over a typical race weekend the pace and the tension gradually quickens until the tempo, like the engines, is at screaming pitch. On race day, there is no room for mistakes. During warm-up everything is checked and re-checked; nothing is left to chance. Nigel Stepney was already noticing the difference in having Ross Brawn and Rory Byrne in place. 'It will take time for it to work fully, but it is a change for the better. Having our own technical people in Maranello makes life easier. We don't have to keep communicating back to England. It was the next step. We couldn't get to the top operating as we were before they arrived. Ross is very good, he's very calm and very English. He has a serious side, but he has a light side as well and both sides work well together.'

The biggest challenge was bringing in modifications for the car while also building up the technical and design office. 'The reliability is better, the car is a bit better, but the biggest difference is that the team is doing a better job in all aspects. It's the fourth year we've had a stabilized team, which has a big effect – not only at the races but also at the factory. People wanted John Barnard, but the distance between us wasn't helpful. Now we are all under one roof and it is better for Jean Todt as he is here in Maranello more and doesn't have to go running off to see what's going on.'

At the track, Brawn takes overall command of Schumacher's car, while Giorgio Ascanelli spends more time

MR FIXIT...
Bernie Ecclestone is the man who has made Formula One visually entertaining and a commercial success. Here he chats to Eddie Irvine and Rod Vickery.

CELEBRATION TIME...
Corinna Schumacher joins in with the team celebrations after her husband's stunning win in the Spanish Grand Prix in 1996.

PROBLEM SOLVING...
The aftermath of Ferrari's disastrous Grand Prix at Silverstone in 1996, with Giorgio Ascanelli and Nigel Stepney trying to work out what went wrong.

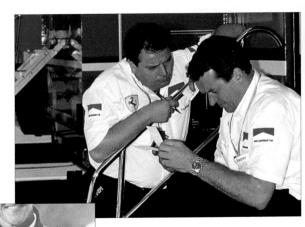

MAN TO MAN...
Ferrari Chairman Luca di Montezemolo discusses with Michael Schumacher the ins and outs of driving a Ferrari Formula One car.

A SCHUMI SALUTE...
'Spa was the best win of the [1996] season,' said Jean Todt. 'It was like a breath of fresh air after all the problems.'

SPEEDY GETAWAY...
Exit from the pits for Eddie Irvine during the 1996 San Marino GP at Imola, where he finished fourth after a poor start.

THE BOSS AND THE BOYS...
Jean Todt, Pino Gozzo and the mechanics celebrate the victory at Monza 96.

BEHIND THE SCENES AT FDD...
Testing technician Alaister Billing operates the single-wheel test rig on the right rear suspension of the car.

THE *TIFOSI*...
The Ferrari fans are part of the culture of Formula One; there is nothing quite like the pride and passion of the *tifosi*.

FREAK OR UNIQUE?...
'I don't want to be treated as special, because I'm not,' says Michael Schumacher.

IN THE FRONT LINE...
A relaxed Ross Brawn, Ferrari's
Technical Director, fields questions
from the world's media.

NEW DESIGNS...
Chief Designer Rory Byrne studies the
monitors during testing.

MELBOURNE MADNESS...
Eddie Irvine's Ferrari clashes with Villeneuve and Herbert at the start of the 1997 Australian Grand Prix. All three drivers retired from the race.

THE ORGANISER...
Chief Press Officer Claudio Berro is calmness personified as he listens into the commentary on the team radio between practice sessions during a Grand Prix weekend.

SUPERIOR CLASS...
Michael Schumacher stays ahead of the opposition.

DOUBLE SUCCESS...
Schumacher and Irvine finish second and
third at Imola in 1997, behind
Heinz-Harald Frentzen.

IT'S THE PITS...
A swift tyre change during pit stops keeps
the Ferraris on the move.

IN THE LEAD...
Race action from the 1997 Formula One World Championship.

WHO'S THE BOSS?...
Michael Schumacher explains the technicalities to Gianni Agnelli.

TRIPLE DELIGHT...
The third victory of 1997 for Schumacher at Magny-Cours in France.

BROTHERLY BASH...
Ralf Schumacher is sent flying by Jordan team-mate Fisichella in 1997, much to the chagrin of brother Michael who tries to take evasive action – but it's too late!

with Irvine. However, these roles aren't cast in stone and if Brawn wants to get involved with Irvine's set-up he will. By the same token, Ascanelli is free to wander over and give the benefit of his experience to Brawn.

For the team this creates a perfect combination – Brawn's steadiness and Ascanelli's ingenuity. As Brawn says, 'What I'm trying to bring to Ferrari is the fact that it's easy to make changes that go backwards as well as forwards. Ferrari is under more pressure than any other team; you can't understand what it is until you experience it. It's unique, there's a constant demand to succeed and consequently a pressure to make changes. If you're not succeeding then the logical thing is to make changes and I feel in the past there may have been occasions when people were forced into changes that were not necessarily for the better. They were made because the team wanted to be seen to be doing things.

'It's very easy to do a lot of work and not go forward. I guess it's the sort of syndrome of keeping your head down and keeping busy, and not putting your head above the parapet. I think that was something Ferrari may have suffered from in the past. If people were to make a criticism of me, it's that perhaps I'm too far the other way and I won't agree to any changes to the car unless I'm certain it's an improvement.'

Schumacher wants to win and he brings pressure on the team to make the modifications to win. That is normal, but last year there was no Brawn to keep the boat steady and changes were made for changes' sake – and to appease Schumacher. As Brawn says, 'Michael is pretty ambitious. He pushes hard to make improvements. His responsibilities are not to judge what should and shouldn't go on the car, but to drive the car as quickly as he can and, quite fairly, put pressure on us to progress. Michael doesn't say "You should put that front wing on the car". He says, "I want to go faster, what are you doing about it?"

'Last year Michael was putting pressure on the team to improve and they definitely made progress, but you need to go forward in a methodical way and ensure that each change is an overall improvement and not just a one-off for a particular track.'

The new *modus operandi* works well, but Giorgio Ascanelli would need time to get used to taking things at a slower pace, even if it now meant he could have more opportunities with his family. He and Nigel Stepney were rather like an old married couple, as Ascanelli pointed out last year, and this year was pretty much the same. A lot of the time they were in each other's shadow, including race day.

● ● ●

Despite Irvine's ninth place on the grid, he finished the San Marino Grand Prix in third place, with team-mate Schumacher second. Both Ferrari drivers on the podium was good for the World Championship but even better for the Constructors' Championship. As usual the pit stops were critical. Schumacher was pleased with his second place, although after the race he admitted, 'I think that maybe the decisive moment was when, by a hair's breath, Frentzen came out in front of me after the first pit stop.'

Ascanelli was also pleased with the second and third finishes, but insists Schumacher could have won. 'Frentzen went out ahead of us by one second in the last pit stop. That's not to say our pit stop was wrong; if it had been there would have been a 10-second difference, but it shows how close it is between winning and coming second.'

With the new season underway, Ascanelli was finding things better with Brawn and Byrne. He is searingly honest about other people and about his own defects. 'We can now walk three steps to Ross' office, say we've got a problem, agree a solution and get it fixed. The reaction time is much better. Ross is a sensible person, he doesn't decide anything on the basis of feelings or emotions. Everything we do now is based on fact. I have to say that I find it extremely pleasant that [long pause] I have a reference point. It wasn't the case last year.

'As for Rory, I enjoyed working with him for a couple of years at Benetton. I like him a lot. He hasn't got a personality full of tantrums like mine! We work together well. He reminds me of a Walt Disney character, I can't remember its name, but it looks like an extra terrestrial, and it goes round naked except for a grass skirt and has big feet. Anyway, the whole point of this is that it is always producing helicopters, houses and so forth from under its grass skirt. It's like Rory in that it has a lot of ideas and solutions. Every time you're lost he pulls something out of the bag.'

But what about talent? 'I believe that Rory is a logical person with a fantastic feel for aerodynamics. He has got the characteristics a designer should have in racing, in that he does the job himself. He's not scared of having a drawing board in his office and drawing lines. Also, when you have a problem he jumps on it and fixes it. He's not a manager and so he's always available.'

THE ENIGMA THAT IS IRVINE
HE KNOWS WHERE IT'S AT IN RACING TERMS

For Irvine, Imola saw his second podium appearance, giving him 10 points in only two races. It was just the tonic he

EDDIE IRVINE

As Ferrari's Number Two driver, Eddie Irvine is getting the 'Schumacher Factor' licked. He keeps his fitness levels high and is supervized by sister Sonia, who is also extremely fit. The pressure of racing and other commitments can take its toll. For example, in the 1996 season, his life was one of non-stop travel. 'I tested before Canada and had things to do with sponsors. I flew from Italy to Dublin and stayed one day in Dublin. Then I flew to New York. From New York I went to Montreal and the Canadian Grand Prix. After the race on the Sunday night I went back to New York and onto Dublin. The next day I flew to France, drove to Magny-Cours, tested for three days, then drove to London again. Two days later I flew to Goodwood. I left there and flew to Dublin, via London, and a couple of days later to Magny-Cours for a 4 pm meeting. Then it was another race weekend...'

Outside of racing, Eddie allowed himself the luxury of buying a second-hand Falcon 10. Many people think a private airplane is the ultimate extravagance but to Irvine it's a necessity. A canny investor, he is pleased that his Hong Kong & Shanghai Bank shares are making him money. He relaxes by reading *The Financial Times* and *The Economist* as well as the business supplements of the major dailies. At home he'll watch the shares on Ceefax and play the guitar. 'My guitar would have to be unplugged for anyone to enjoy listening to it,' he says. 'I like nothing better than sitting at home by myself looking at the stocks and shares and trying to figure out *Sunday, Bloody Sunday* on the guitar.'

needed after last year's fiasco. 'I was able to start well and carry on through the field to bring another four points to Ferrari, which is a great satisfaction.' The race was also satisfying for tyre manufacturer Goodyear, which had been criticized by Luca di Montezemolo before the race. He had declared, 'I think it has fallen asleep and needs to be shaken up. But I have no doubt that we shall be able to recuperate.' This dig at Goodyear came after Bridgestone had demonstrated its skills with wet tyres. Goodyear replied with all three podium places going to drivers on its tyres.

Back at Maranello the day after the race, fans — predominantly German — poured into the souvenir shops and meandered round the town as though on some kind of religious pilgrimage. Paolo Bortolai, who is in charge of La Galleria, the Ferrari museum and shop, has never seen anything like it. He reckoned that there were 30 to 40 per cent more people in 1997 than in 1996. 'Our record number of visitors in one day is 1,267 and 70 per cent of our visitors are foreign. We are also part of the school visits programme, so lots of schools bring their kids to see Maranello and Ferrari. It's almost part of the curriculum.'

Like Ferrari, of which it is a part, La Galleria exudes style and elegance. From the smallest red leather keyrings and yellow cardboard tubs of matches to the tan leather briefcases and racing hats, Italian style and panache is in evidence. Part of the reason for the resurgence in hope at Ferrari is Eddie Irvine's improved form. At Imola he was on the podium for the second time in four races. Last year Schumacher managed three wins, but Irvine's season was more or less a disaster — a third, two fifths and a fourth.

One of the things in his favour is that unlike most of Schumacher's previous team-mates, Irvine did not whinge

NIGEL STEPNEY'S RACE DAY AT IMOLA

6.30 am: 'We're at the track (three hours before warm-up). We push two of the cars down to scrutineering to make sure they are within regulations. We practise re-fuelling, tyre changes and nose changes.'

7.30 am: The team uses a rota system for breakfast. 'I wander back to the pits and check on progress.'

8.00 am: The cars are back from scrutineering. 'We have to prepare to start-up the engines. We put fuel in for the morning warm-up.'

8.30–

9.30 am: 'The hour before warm-up is busy as it is a wet warm-up, so we have to change the settings and tyres etc. We put more fuel in for the wet changes, and we have to do a bit of work on the tyres and make sure the wet tyres were in the warm-up blankets. We put more wing on the T-car, and Schumacher leaves his race car the same on dry settings. We swap around two or three times.'

10.00 am: Warm-up is over and there have been no major problems.

12.30 pm: 'We start to put dry settings on the car, then we put on our fireproof overalls. If it's a hot race we end up like a wet sponge.'

1.30 pm: 'The pit lane opens and the cars leave for two or three laps of warm-up. They go out on wet tyres, then come back through the pit lane to change to slicks and go to the grid.'

1.40–
1.45 pm: 'We set up the area for re-fuelling and tyre changes.
We are ready in case it rains again on the formation lap.

2.00 pm: 'We return to the pits as the race starts. During the race
we're on the radio. The engine guys tell us the fuel
consumption and the temperatures plus how much fuel
to put in the car for the next pit stop. A good pit stop is
a combination of things including the driver. It's very
satisfying when you get it right as it's 20 people
working together in the space of seven to eight seconds.'

4.00 pm: 'The race has finished, but we have to go into panic
mode and get all the equipment into the garage. It's a
bit like facing a herd of stampeding elephants as the
fans rush down the pit lane. The cars go in for
scrutineering and the FIA can check whatever it wants
to check. We start packing the material away, which took
a little longer at Imola as we couldn't move for people!
All members of the team have certain roles. There is a
post-race debrief with the drivers, and the mechanics do
their post-race checks of the engine, brakes and fuel
consumption. Then everyone helps pack up the equipment.
It takes us about four hours to pack away everything.'

8.00 pm: 'We're hungry! We're only an hour away from home at
Imola so we go to eat and let the traffic ease before
driving home.'

during his awful 1996 season. He just got on with things and refused to lay the blame on other people. Everyone knew he wasn't getting the testing or the new parts, but he didn't underline the fact every five minutes.

There is a lot more to Irvine than his 'Irish lad having a good time' reputation suggests, or maybe that is just a convenient cover. He knows where it's at in racing terms and he's also very bright with a good grasp of financial know-how in relation to stocks and shares. In addition to this, he also does a good job for the team's sponsors, which is important as Schumacher, since the birth of his daughter, has cut back on his off-track commitments. However, the one thing Irvine has no time for is people who are unprofessional in their dealings with him. In the case of the media this means journalists who ask what he considers to be stupid or ill-prepared questions.

It turned out that one of his main problems last year had been his seat. For most of the time it wasn't just uncomfortable, but sheer agony. 'I was getting out of the car in real pain. I was driving round having to move my legs as I was in such pain. We tried to understand what the problem was and the first time we sorted it out was in Argentina this year. Although we haven't fixed it completely, it's not an issue anymore. I'm not driving around thinking "Jesus, my back's killing me!"'

Irvine was also enjoying a better relationship with his race engineer, Luca Baldisserri. Luca is a quiet, bespectacled, serious individual who, like most race engineers, is fiercely loyal to his driver. 'It's important to have a good rapport with the driver. It's important to be friends, as if you are too professional you lose something; you have to understand what he is saying, by also understanding what he *isn't* saying. We had a difficult year, but we talked things over in the winter and decided to give it another go. We were helped by Ross who sat us both down and sorted it out.

'One of Eddie's main problems last year was lack of testing. He needs more stability in the corners, he hates oversteer. The car tended to be unstable in the entry of the corner and so his times would go up. The car went very well in Argentina this year, that was the best moment.' The worst race was undoubtedly Monaco last year. 'There was lack of understanding between us. He came into the pits pointing downwards. We'd changed the nose before we realized he wanted us to do up his seat belts, which he had undone when going off the track earlier. Not our best moment!'

Baldisserri also pays tribute to Ross Brawn. 'He has brought tranquillity and organization, especially on the technical side. He is much more methodical; now everything is planned, so we do not arrive [at races] at the last moment with bits that haven't been tried.'

Ignazio Lunetta, Schumacher's race engineer, was also a happier man. He and Schumacher were enjoying a close and mutually respectful relationship. Schumacher says of him, 'He's a fantastic guy. I like him very, very much. He's a good human being and a good engineer. When he's under stress he gets a bit wound up but he is the right man to have by my side.'

Lunetta was also finding Schumacher easier to handle. 'He's a bit more relaxed and trusts us more, which is nice. I enjoy working with him. Working with the best is always very satisfying, and it keeps you on your toes.' So far, the 1997 season was turning out to be easier than 1996. 'It's a better car, faster and easier to work with. We need more performance from it and more grip, but progress is good.'

Lunetta also appreciates Brawn. 'He's brought method to the team. We are less impulsive. Ross protects us from the outside. We don't see the chairman of Ferrari around the factory as much as we used to do. Although it's always a pleasure to see the chairman, at our level we shouldn't have direct contact.'

Just as the two race engineers were getting down to discussing the finer points of racing, Rory Byrne popped his head round the door. Born in Pretoria, South Africa, he had been in England in the motor racing industry since 1973. In 1994 and 1995 he won the World Championship with Michael Schumacher. At the end of 1996 he decided to leave Benetton and retire to open a scuba diving school in Thailand, where he lived with his Thai girlfriend. But after a few months of sailing the blue waters and living in the sunshine he was back in Europe. 'I was attracted to the challenge. Ferrari is the most famous team and attempting to win the Championship after nearly 20 years was too good to turn down,' he says.

● ● ●

There was an atmosphere of quiet satisfaction throughout the team that things were getting better. And just to prove that, the next stop was Monte Carlo.

CHAPTER SIX

Winning Ways

'When you looked up at the slopes
overlooking the circuit, there was just
a sea of red flags and red caps, even in
the appalling weather conditions.'

Ross Brawn
Ferrari Technical Director, 1997

Prince Albert of Monaco was in his private rooms overlooking the harbour at the Palace. Refreshingly normal with no airs or graces, Albert is the same as any motor racing fan, except he is a Prince and therefore has access that most of us can only dream about.

Born in 1958, the first race he can recall was in 1965, when he was seven years old. 'I remember being close to the track, feeling the noise and noticing the smells that are a part of motor racing. Graham Hill won and I'll never forget the distinctive, piercing sound of the engine.' The Ferrari pit was in front of him and having watched the comings and goings of the pit lane, he was entranced. 'In 1967 I was fascinated by the Sharknose; it was the neatest thing I'd ever seen.' The other great thing about Ferrari was the food. 'We always managed to get invited to eat at Ferrari, it had the best pasta I'd ever tasted.'

There were many occasions for Prince Albert to get better acquainted with his new love. The John Frankenheimer film *Grand Prix* was filmed partly in Monaco, and Albert was able to mix with the stars and their cars. He also made friends with the drivers like Clay Regazzoni, Michele Alboreto (who had to take the pressure of being an Italian driver driving for Ferrari), and Gilles Villeneuve, one of Prince Albert's favourites and a driver who 'represented motor racing through his spirit, guts and style of driving'.

Of the modern drivers Prince Albert says, 'I like Nigel Mansell who I got to know and admire. Michael Schumacher is a driver I respect for his skill and determination. He has the German ability to focus, although he is rather cold-blooded.'

Even for Royal princes, Ferrari has an enigmatic, almost mystical appeal, as does its founder Enzo Ferrari. 'There is something magical about Ferrari, it is a big part of motor racing. I remember Enzo Ferrari as an intimidating, almost god-like figure. He was an incredible man, an imposing figure with a big personality.'

Back down among the mortals, the next stop was the Hotel de Paris where David and Chris Mills were hosting their annual exhibition of motor racing art by painter Alan Fearnley. It was the 10th anniversary of the show and the best so far. Alan is a romantic as well as being a stickler for detail and the combination produces some beautiful, colourful paintings that capture the spirit of motor racing, from the 1950s to the modern era.

Next on the agenda was the Asprey Party at the Hotel Riviera in St Jean Cap-Ferrat. Edward Asprey was, as usual, a great host and most of the in-crowd were present. Court painter Andrew Vicari, who is famous for his larger-than-life paintings of people like General de Gaulle and Princess Caroline, was among the guests, as was rising Hollywood star Mark Thomas.

For Asprey, the Grands Prix are a way of entertaining guests, never less than 25 and up to 60, at Monaco. These privileged few are flown out to the venues, put up in the best hotels and taken to the track, where they are entertained in the Paddock Club in high style, and treated to pit tours to observe the team and get a little closer to the action. It's Asprey's way of saying 'Thank you' to good clients. In 1997, over 400 Asprey guests visited the Grands Prix. They are always impressed with what they see, particularly the pits. As Edward Asprey once said, 'Doctors liken the pits to an operating table, and engineers are impressed by seeing the finest skills, quality, expertise and telemetry in action.'

It hadn't been too long since Edward had his first taste behind the wheel of a Ferrari. 'I had lunch with Nicholas

Lancaster, the chairman and managing director of HR Owen, and he offered me a Ferrari car to drive, so I took him up on the offer when my wife Christina and I were going away for the weekend. The car was a 355 GTS and if it was mine my licence would last a week! The performance is outstanding and what was surprising was how easy it is to drive from a technical point of view. I've driven high performance sport cars and they can be very difficult, but the Ferrari was easy. You can put it in sixth gear at 2,000 revs, put your foot down and glide away. Sheer magic.'

THE RAIN MASTER
SCHUMACHER PROVES HE IS SIMPLY THE BEST

Meanwhile in Monte Carlo, the weather was changeable. Black clouds kept rolling off the mountains that surround Monaco, and rain looked likely. Ferrari's in-house weatherman, Pino Gozzo, spent the entire weekend studying the sky with a worried look on his face. As the Williams team was about to demonstrate, you can make complete idiots of yourselves if you take the wrong decision on car and tyre set-up. The other reason Pino looked so worried was because he'd already had a similar experience in the past. 'It was here at Monaco. I'd just finished giving a weather update in the briefing meeting a few minutes before the pit lane opened. It was not raining and it was not expected to rain, and just as I finished telling everyone that, the heaven's opened and the worst storm for years hit us! Surprisingly enough, I am still the weather expert.'

Schumacher missed pole position by 19/1,000ths of a second, to Frentzen in the Williams. 'I was a bit surprised at the time I did. I thought I could go faster after the morning session, but not by that much. I thought the others would also be a lot faster. It leaves me pretty confident for a podium finish tomorrow.'

Half an hour before the race was due to start, the sky darkened and the rain began. Williams Renault had information that it would clear up and then be showery, so Frentzen and Villeneuve appeared in the pouring rain on slicks. As Harvey Postlethwaite of Tyrrell said, 'We have a simple policy here: if it is raining we put on wet tyres.'

Schumacher, meanwhile, was seen studying two cars, his own and the T-car (the team's spare car), and then selecting the T-car, which had been set up for the wet, to race in. Ross Brawn takes up the story: 'Michael had two different set-ups on two different cars, one was specifically set up for the wet and one for dry conditions. Before the race Michael went out and had a look at the track to see if it was wet enough to utilize the car that was set up for the wet. It was him and him only who made that decision and I think that is correct as he was the only one who would know what the track was like.'

Schumacher was on intermediate tyres which, considering the downpour, was amazing. Most of the other cars were slipping and sliding all over the place. He completed his opening lap six-and-a-half seconds ahead of anyone else; after 10 laps he was in the lead by nearly half a minute and it increased until he settled into a nice, 70-second lead with which to end the race. There was simply no one else who was even close. His incredible performance in the rain at Spain last year was magic to watch, and if anyone had thought it was a one-off, Schumacher proved once again that he is simply the best. Give him a half-decent, reliable car and he'll beat anyone; give him a half-decent, reliable car in the wet and he'll make the rest look like amateurs.

However, although he was having a great race, the shadow of his *faux pas* during the first lap of last year's race was never far away. Every time he passed the barrier where he'd gone off he admitted, 'I kept thinking "Shit, I'll have to be extra careful after last year."'

There was one heart-stopping moment when Schumacher ran off the track into the escape road at Ste Dévote. Some people said he probably nodded off. His reason was more down to earth. 'I locked the front wheel. Maybe I could have made it round the corner, but I decided not to take the risk and to do a detour round the escape road.'

For the team it was the fourth win with Schumacher. But for Ross Brawn it was his first. 'It was pretty special, even though it's not my car, it's John's [Barnard] car. We've managed to consolidate and improve it, but it will feel better when it is actually my car that wins. Having said that, it's still an incredible experience. It reinforces the fact that Ferrari is the biggest team in Formula One. When you looked up at the slopes overlooking the circuit, there was just a sea of red flags and red caps, even in the appalling weather conditions.'

For the first time since 1989, Ferrari led the Drivers' Championship as well as the Constructors' Championship. However, both Schumacher and Team Director Jean Todt remained cautious. Schumacher said, 'There are still 12 races to go. We have been fairly lucky so far because Williams has had certain problems which have made us jump in front of them.' Todt was equally pragmatic. 'We have been trying to achieve the position to fight for the Championship for four years, and we have to be very careful to keep our heads clear and know where we are.'

It was a great win for Schumacher but it was also an exceptional third place for his team-mate Eddie Irvine, who had moved up the field from 15th. The race strategy of one pit stop worked to perfection. Irvine might have been able to go the whole distance without stopping as the rain meant the race ended at the maximum two-hour mark, 16 laps early. However, he knew it would be difficult to clinch second, so it was decided to consolidate his third place by changing the tyres and putting in a little fuel. It was a good day for teamwork and tangible evidence that progress was being made.

It is easy to put it all down to Ross Brawn, but the team has been built up over four years, a time during which stability and consistency had been sought and now, at Monaco, achieved. However, the celebrations in the Ferrari motorhome were muted compared to the wild happiness at the Stewart motorhome after the team's driver Rubens Barrichello came second. For a new team it was the ecstasy of the first taste of near victory. For the grand dame of Formula One, it was a more laid back affair, although things hotted up after the race when the team hit the celebrated night spot, Jimmy's, staying until dawn the next day. Ross Brawn, shattered by the emotion and sheer hard work, left the others at 1 am. Nigel Stepney led the partying until breakfast time when everyone dragged themselves back to the hotel.

There wasn't time to breathe before testing at Barcelona and getting ready for the Spanish Grand Prix. The Ferrari 310B is not suited to Barcelona's Circuit de Catalunya, where the long curves cause problems for the car.

Schumacher doesn't understand exactly why this should be so, but he tries to explain the effects. 'Perhaps it is the long corners. You build up a lot of tyre temperature and that hurts us. It's also a balance problem. In these types of long corner, you need good balance from the beginning to the end, and we're not that good there.'

Some of the main chit-chat away from the track centred on Schumacher's debut in a Swiss third division football match. He played for Aubonne FC before the Grand Prix, but it wasn't a huge success. He admitted, 'It proved to me that I should stay where I am and not go in other directions. I was in the wrong position for me [he was playing centre forward], but I was not playing well – I missed a goal.' There were mumblings about contracts forbidding dangerous sports, but when you're Michael Schumacher you can do pretty well what you like.

After the first day's practice in Barcelona, tyre wear was already posing a problem – not just for Ferrari but for all the other Goodyear runners, too. Irvine thought he might pick up a point or two, but in qualifying both Ferraris were off the pace with Schumacher achieving seventh position after a massive engine blow-up and Irvine 11th.

Rain threatened on race morning and for one glorious moment it looked like it could be a re-run of 1996. No such luck and the Ferraris had a difficult race due to tyre blistering. Schumacher had to stop on lap 12 to change his tyres, and after that the race strategy was changed from two to three pit stops, with additional stops on laps 30 and 46. Irvine was also originally on a two-stop strategy which was extended to three; he came in on lap 19, made an early second stop on lap 28, and then a final visit to the pits on lap 49.

Schumacher's two points for finishing fifth kept Ferrari in the lead in the Constructors' Championship by one point. After his three good races in Argentina, Imola and Monaco, Irvine had a less than remarkable race. Not only did he finish a lowly 12th but he was also given a 10-second stop–go penalty for blocking second-place Olivier Panis, who was chasing eventual race winner Villeneuve. Irvine wasn't happy, as he felt it was unfair. He claimed that he couldn't see a thing due to the debris coming from Damon Hill's car, and he thought the flag was for Trulli who was holding up both him and Verstappen.

TESTING TIMES
AND THEN THERE IS ANOTHER SESSION

Former Ferrari personnel manager (now team manager) Stefano Domenicali is under constant pressure to ensure the team members are where they should be with everything they should have. 'In May, June and July we have an incredibly heavy test programme,' says Domenicali. 'After Imola, Schumacher and Irvine tested at Fiorano, on the Friday Schumacher had an extra test day, then on Saturday there was the shakedown (when the set-up for the race is checked and it is verified there are no major failures or problems) for the cars that were going to Monaco.

'Immediately after Monaco we have a three-day test at Barcelona, on the Monday after that the shakedown for Spain. After Spain a three-day test at Silverstone, followed by the celebrations and exhibitions in Rome, Modena and Maranello for Ferrari's 50th anniversary. Immediately after that we all leave for Canada. The Monday after Canada there is another test session at Magny-Cours for three days. On the Monday after that, the shakedown for Magny-Cours. Immediately after Magny-Cours there is a three-day test at Silverstone. After Silverstone a three-day test at Monza, following three days at Fiorano, and so on...'

Gigi Mazzola, who leads the Ferrari test team, had already noticed a change at Ferrari with Ross Brawn's presence. 'There's more organization and a more detailed programme, so when we are testing we know exactly what we have to do during the day. Michael [Schumacher] fits in very well with this philosophy as he's a very organized guy. He sticks to the plan and we work through all the items we have to test. Everything has improved because of Ross. Michael's contribution is better as it's more logical.'

It's not the case that Ferrari understands Schumacher better this year than last. As Mazzola points out, 'You have to enter into the driver's mentality very quickly. You might get more feeling for him after three or four years, but you will not know him better than after two months.'

Irvine has more input this year as there are two test cars and, of course, the car is more reliable. 'The situation is easier for Eddie as he has the opportunity to test. I think he did a pretty good job during winter testing. I think he's stronger physically and fitter. As soon as the driver can test, he can try out different options on the car, the handling, the setting-up of the engine or brakes. That means that when he goes into the race weekend he already knows what he has to do.'

The test at Silverstone after the Spanish GP was the first time Ferrari had tested at the British track for many years. Up until this year each team had to keep to its designated track – in Ferrari's case Monza. Now that FOCA has organized general testing, which gives the less well-off teams the chance to compete with the big boys, the circuit advantage has evened out.

Test days are inevitably peppered with pauses as crashed cars are removed from the track. Schumacher went off on the Wednesday of testing when his rear suspension broke as he was taking a corner at 200 kilometres an hour. But in tests these things happen. As Mazzola explains, 'In a test you develop new things, try new technology, make something lighter or make something different, or you want to see how long those parts will stay together. If you want to see how long the suspension lasts you keep running the car and checking all the time, until it wears out. In either case you can have failure, either because the part is new or because it is at the end of its life. These things have to happen *during* the test, not *at* the race.'

At Silverstone the Ferrari test team had set about solving the problem of mechanical grip. 'Basically we need more mechanical grip. The car is missing mechanical grip in the slow part of the corner. A long corner is difficult, a short corner is all right. It depends on the circuit: it's all right at Imola, difficult at Monaco. Spain is difficult for corners and tyres.'

As with the race team, there is more optimism this year among the test team. The car still needs some modifications but Ferrari is picking up points and this means that team members are working well and, of course, there is that invaluable 'x' factor – Schumacher. Having the best driver makes a lot of difference, both in terms of actual results and in the more intangible feeling of morale. Both were on the way up at Ferrari.

The next race on the calendar was Canada, but before that were the celebrations for Ferrari's 50th anniversary. Starting in Rome and ending in Modena and Maranello it was going to be one hell of a party.

FIFTY GOLDEN YEARS
THE SPIRIT OF ENZO FERRARI WAS DEFINITELY PRESENT

Ferrari began its 50th anniversary celebrations in Rome to coincide with its first victory at the Caracalla circuit on the 25 May 1947. This venue was chosen despite the fact that Enzo Ferrari never had much to do with Rome, having visited the city only once in 1935 for a minor race. Coming from the north he regarded the Italian capital as full of bureaucrats, with a tendency for disorganization. Having said this, he remained fascinated with the city and was always happy to hear tales and gossip from the friends and associates who came to visit him from Rome.

Fifty years later, almost to the day, the great and the good gathered to see an exhibition of Ferrari cars, old and modern, including the F310Bs of Michael Schumacher and Eddie Irvine. Some 270 Ferraris owned by collectors throughout the world were gathered at the Marble Stadium, which is near the Olympic Stadium and better known for being the host of the Italian Open Tennis Championship.

The President of Italy, Oscar Luigi Scalfaro, Vice-President Walter Veltroni, the Mayor of Rome, Francesco Rutelli, Fiat boss Gianni Agnelli and Ferrari Chairman Luca di Montezemolo, among others, attended the opening ceremony to start the celebrations that would end the following weekend with a spectacular fireworks show and concert at Modena.

An emotional Montezemolo, who himself would be 50 on 31 August 1997, thanked everyone for participating and admitted that for the first time in his life he'd asked the drivers to drive slowly to the Caracalla, across the city of Rome. 'I'll never make this request again!' he joked.

After the official speeches were made, the President and Vice-President of Italy, followed by the Mayor, Agnelli and Montezemolo, all hurried over to look at the cars first hand, and live out their boyhood dreams. Included in the line up was the only Ferrari police car (in service in the 1960s), complete with blue lamp, a huge radio and a still working siren! While the President of Italy was with the police car, the Vice-President was gazing at Gilles Villeneuve's old Formula One car and wondering how anyone could fit inside it. Then, like a kid in a toy shop, his attention was diverted by the sight of the very first Ferrari, the Auto Avio, which was a prototype car produced in the 1940s.

Slowly the drivers came forward once more to pay homage to their cars. The Argentinian driver Jose Froilan Gonzalez, the 'Pampas Bull', bent down to kiss the bonnet of his car, while Phil Hill admired his, which was the first Ferrari single-seater with a rear-mounted engine, and with which he won the Formula One World Championship in 1961, the first American to do so. Then the ex-Ferrari drivers, along with the current two, Schumacher and Irvine, got together to pose for the family album – but the real stars of the show were the cars.

Bearing in mind this was essentially a weekend for the Ferrari owners and collectors, thousands of people braved the weather (which went from baking hot to pouring rain) to catch the merest glance of a car that represents the best of Italy. But the unpredictable weather failed to dampen spirits and Montezemolo laughed declaring, 'I'd have preferred to have the rain in Spain.'

For the men of Maranello it was an experience that took them out of the narrow world of Formula One and showed them the intense emotions that the name Ferrari arouses in ordinary people.

As Ignazio Lunetta says, 'It was a wonderful party atmosphere in Rome. I love the city and to take Ferrari there was a dream. There were so many people, that in moments like these you realize just how much Ferrari means to them and how important it is. We don't have much contact with the general public, so it is only when you come to somewhere like Rome for the 50th anniversary that you realize the intensity of this passion.'

Michael Schumacher was deep in conversation with Jody Scheckter, who had won the World Championship for Ferrari in 1979. Scheckter admitted that when he drove for the team he didn't understand what it meant to be a Ferrari driver and represent not only a name but also the whole of Italy. But as time passes and he is constantly remembered as the last Ferrari driver to win the World Championship, he now understands. With generosity he commented, 'I'll be delighted when Michael has taken over this role.'

Schumacher was also experiencing what Ferrari means to Italy and the fact that nothing, not a Williams nor a Benetton, nor any other car can excite and tantalize like a Ferrari. 'It really is great being a Ferrari driver and I'll give 100 per cent to taking over from Scheckter as soon as possible.'

The spirit of Enzo Ferrari was very definitely present. Strong, determined and obstinate, he was known to manage his staff and the people he came across in a manner that would produce the best results for the company. John Surtees remembers his most exciting moments when he won two Grands Prix with a six-cylinder engine and Enzo Ferrari said, 'I won't pay you a lot, as being a Ferrari driver means you'll be able to get discounts everywhere.' Like Frank Williams, he never made the driver more important than the car.

The 270 cars drove round the Coliseum and the Circo Massimo to create scenes that will never be repeated. Member of the public were enchanted, but the excitement reached a crescendo when Schumacher and Irvine climbed into their cars to drive round Caracalla. Instead of driving sedately, they put on a show, overtaking and screaming round the track to the delight of the crowds, and then rounding it off with a pit stop to change tyres before they finished with a wave to the fans for whom the occasion might have been their only chance to glimpse a Formula One car.

After Rome the Ferrari cortège travelled to Fiorano. The cars followed the same road as the famous Mille Miglia (1,000 mile) race with pit stops in Siena and Florence. Once in the north there were more celebrations. The streets of Modena were decorated with large graphics that reproduced the old Ferrari headquarters in viale Trento and Trieste, Enzo Ferrari's house and Largo Garibaldi where the times of the Mille Miglia were posted.

Under the guidance of Antonio Ghini, both Claudio Berro and Stefano Domenicali had organized most of the event – a responsibility that, in parallel with their normal jobs, involved many long days and short nights. At the end of the week they were both exhausted, with barely time to pause before the Grand Prix circus called them to Canada.

But for a short time, Ferrari once more dominated the cities that formed the character of its creator, Enzo Ferrari. In Maranello, people joined in with the celebrations as though they were all shareholders or personal friends. Council offices, banks, schools, cafés, green grocers and supermarkets were all covered in photos of old races; even the taxi drivers drove around with the prancing horse displayed in their windows.

On Saturday 7 June the Ferrari party culminated in an evening show that eclipsed all others. Edward Asprey was knocked out by the sheer enormity of the entertainment. 'There were fireworks on a scale that I've never seen before; it was as I imagine the 21st-century celebrations will be. It was absolutely fantastic – the show and the music. It was tangible evidence of the absolute power of Ferrari to entice and seduce anyone who comes into contact with the cars and the history. It was a special honour to be part of the Ferrari family and experience history in the making. I don't think I'll be around for the 100-year celebrations so I'm glad I was here for the 50-year ones!'

The collectors, friends and fans all mingled with one another, drinking in the rare atmosphere of shared hopes and dreams. Montezemolo was hailed the hero who was slowly but surely bringing the prancing horse back to full health. Although he tried to play down the chances of Schumacher winning the World Championship in 1997, it was the only question on many people's lips. No longer if or maybe, but when. If Schumacher could win the Championship in the 50th year of the prancing horse after a drought of 18 years he would be given the freedom of the country, never mind the city. There had been many crushed dreams during these last barren years. Now the people wanted victory. As if part of the master plan, their faith in the future was about to be given a massive injection of hope in Canada, which was host to the second Schumacher victory of the year.

CANADA
THE NIGHTMARE SCENARIO

The 1997 Canadian Grand Prix was a strange affair. Schumacher was declared the winner, but it was a hollow victory. The race had been stopped after Frenchman Olivier Panis had crashed his Prost car heavily into the barriers, breaking both legs. That aside, Schumacher really owed his victory to David Coulthard's clutch problems, which delayed the McLaren in the pits — coincidentally at the same time as Panis's accident. Prior to this pit stop, Coulthard had been leading the race.

When Panis remained motionless, it brought back heart-stopping memories, memories of the tragic day on 1 May 1994 when the great Ayrton Senna perished in a collision with a barrier wall during the San Marino Grand Prix.

Ferrari's Chief Engineer Giorgio Ascanelli had been Senna's race engineer some years earlier at McLaren, and the accident triggered some powerful emotions for him. 'The victory in

Canada was not happy. It was clouded by the Panis issue. When a race is stopped, you always think the worst. From what we could see from the television monitors, it wasn't good. This is always a worry and the win suddenly didn't matter at all. The bottom line is that it's my job to ensure the safe running of the cars. When something goes wrong, your worst fears come out.

'I am never relaxed when the car is on the track. There is always something that can happen. The unpredictable can happen or the predictable when you've simply been negligent. It happens, although sometimes the consequences are small.'

This is a nightmare scenario for Ascanelli and he recalls a particular incident which highlighted his fears. 'I remember something that happened not to me, but it could have done. It was the first practice session for the 1994 British Grand Prix. Hill was on the third corner when both wishbones flopped out of the chassis. They had not been fitted correctly. People do make mistakes. We are only human. Drivers can make mistakes in over-estimating their ability and the car's capacity and have an accident. A mechanic who is probably working until 4 am and then starting again at 6.30 am after an hour's sleep can make mistakes. This is understandable. But if something goes wrong, the first thing you ask is, "What did I do wrong?" It's the nature of the job and part of being the person responsible for the team at the track.'

Schumacher, after his pole position and race victory, was in subdued mood, barely lifting the trophy up to the crowds and leaving the unopened bottles of champagne at his feet. But the important thing was that his ambition was back. His race engineer Ignazio Lunetta says, 'Michael's more motivated. He's always very attentive, but when his level of attentiveness goes up even further, you know he is on the case. After Barcelona he was a bit down, but after Canada he was back on top.'

The pragmatic Nigel Stepney put the whole thing in context: 'Panis's accident is not the way to win points, but 10 points is 10 points. We expected to do well but we didn't expect pole position in qualifying. We struggled a bit with the tyres; we opted for the hardest type but they were still too soft.'

So, after Canada, Schumacher was still leading Villeneuve in the Drivers' Championship by seven points, and Ferrari was eight points clear of its nearest rival Williams in the Constructors' Championship. The basic fact of life was that Villeneuve had thrown it away on his home turf because of an unforced error on the second lap. As Stepney said dismissively, 'He tried to drive like Schumacher.' Eddie Irvine was not having a great time either, but for different reasons. He was off the pace in qualifying and out of the race on the first lap due to no fault of his own. McLaren driver Mika Hakkinen had clashed with Panis's Prost and Irvine was the victim as he collided with Mika's nose cone.

The Irishman wasn't happy. 'This was the worst race for me in terms of qualifying. I really felt I was going to qualify well in Canada. The car was good all week. But come qualifying it all just fell apart. I don't know whether I fell apart, but I just couldn't brake late and Canada is all about braking late.

'I didn't have the confidence for some reason. It was very depressing. I just don't understand it. It may be a psychological reason but it becomes physical when qualifying in the Ferrari. There is some feeling I'm getting from the car when I'm out qualifying that I don't like. I feel it's going to bite me. Maybe I'm overbraking, trying to push too hard or something like that.'

Maybe Schumacher's times have some bearing. Irvine says, 'Maybe he does have a negative effect on you when you see these amazing times and you think "I must push harder", when in effect you don't have to or you just try too hard and it becomes less natural.'

Irvine gives a good performance as a laid back, 'nothing bothers me' type character. The truth is, like anyone who is competing at the top level in their chosen sport, he's ambitious, focused and craves the taste of victory, so the race was a big disappointment. 'I thought I'd have a good race. I didn't have a tyre blistering problem in Canada. I was going round the outside of everyone and it was the right thing to do as everyone was bunched up on the inside. I was on the outside thinking "Fantastic". The next thing I knew a piece of someone's car came flying out of nowhere and just went underneath the rear wheel, flicked me round and cut the engine. That was it. The end of my race. I was on a one-stop race strategy. I was sure of the podium. I was really very confident and it all went wrong.'

LOOKING AHEAD
THERE WAS A PROGRAMME OF MODIFICATIONS

After Canada the team went to test at the French circuit at Magny-Cours, home to the next race, and gave the new grooved tyres, which were due to be used during the 1998 season, their first outing.

The new regulations for 1998 were wide ranging and aimed at reducing speeds. There were fierce discussions about them. On the one hand, drivers like Jacques Villeneuve believed that they would be unnecessary because speed and danger are part of the thrill of Formula One; on the other, FIA boss Max Mosley defended the decision to reduce speed: 'If you continue to go 250 kilometres an hour through a corner, there is more risk of an accident as experience shows this is the moment of greatest danger. Common sense dictates that these speeds must be reduced. There are 16 corners that have been identified as dangerous in Formula One; if we can reduce speeds by three seconds a lap this will be cut by half to eight. If we don't do this there will be a big accident. Only in this way can we preserve great corners like Eau Rouge at Spa [in Belgium]. My job is to make sure that the Grand Prix drivers survive past their retirement age, and the best way of doing this is with grooved tyres.'

Schumacher had his own views on grooved tyres. 'The speed of entry into the corners is the same, it is the mid and exit points that are slower. As expected there is less grip, as the relationship of grip to power is different. With the current car they reduce the speed by about five seconds a lap. With next year's car it will be different and we'll have to see.'

Schumacher's greatest desire was to see an increase in overtaking possibilities which would not only be more interesting for the drivers but also offer more entertainment for the crowds. 'They haven't found the rules to get racing back to what it was in the 1970s and 80s, and we should at least be able to overtake somehow. I would like a genuine opportunity to race and overtake. That's why I do winter karting as I get satisfaction that I don't get through the year.'

Ross Brawn was taking the new regulation changes in his stride. 'We have to accept that we can't keep making the cars go faster and faster. The gain in times comes from braking and cornering. As there is little progress in engine power, we're braking harder and going through corners faster. This means the velocity of the car in corners is higher, so if it does leave the track it will travel further. I think something was necessary and I think grooved tyres were one solution.

'The drivers don't like the fact that they don't have as much grip as they used to with the old tyres. Whether you can reduce the grip in a way that makes the car driver friendly is debatable. I think it is one solution that is in place and we have to work with it. Some drivers have a different view and as they drive the cars, they know better than me. Villeneuve says it reduces the skill level, but I don't understand that. If you use wet conditions as an example, the driver skill comes to the fore and technology takes a back seat. I think it will put more emphasis on driver skill. Time will tell.'

Giorgio Ascanelli reflects Enzo Ferrari's philosophy. 'Enzo Ferrari said that to go fast you need more power, less drag, more downforce, less weight and better brakes. There is no other secret. The new grooved tyres will affect brakes by limiting the braking ability of the car; you will have less powerful, smaller brakes. Brakes are a big part of the basics of a Formula One car. It is one of the reasons we went better in Imola than in other places. We have, I believe, a brake advantage and Imola is heavy on brakes.'

Ross Brawn had been working with Ferrari for six months and it seemed a good time to reflect on the main differences between Benetton and Ferrari, and discuss some of the new modifications coming on line. 'Benetton has Flavio Briatore who is team principal and plays a much more entrepreneurial role than Jean Todt does here. Jean is much more of a hands-on manager, and much more involved in the every-day working of the company. This is a good thing as long as it's someone who knows what they are doing, and Jean does. For Flavio to get involved with the every-day running of the company would have been a mistake, that's not his strength. I think I can work quite well within each system.

'With Flavio there was complete freedom as he didn't get involved with the technical side. His real involvement was assessing the results and discussing the funding. Jean has much more involvement with the general running of the company, but he gives more support. When things are difficult Jean is there to support you and help fix it. I had Flavio's support but in a different way – it was more a no-interference support.'

Regarding strengths and weaknesses, according to Brawn the design side of Ferrari was still not up to strength, although it was coming up to speed and he was expecting it to be as good as, if not better than, Benetton. 'We have some very good people, but we need to consolidate a little more, get the design team established and then take on the world!'

When John Barnard delivered the new car in January 1997, there were various modifications planned including a new gearbox, which had now been put on hold. As Brawn says, 'We have rolled the new gearbox into next year's [1998] programme. I didn't think it was worth it in terms of performance gain. Every team is limited from a resources point of view as to what they can and can't do. In addition to this we have a new engine next year which is different enough to require another gearbox. That would have meant three different gearboxes in the space of a year, which is not something you'd do without considerable thought.'

Shell was also in the process of looking at different gearbox oils in order to improve the efficiency of the gearbox and hopefully lower its running temperature. The gearbox has important potential in the fight to get more power for the car to go faster. It is one of the chief absorbers of power in the mechanical system. A 90 per cent efficient gearbox will still be absorbing 70-plus horsepower from a modern F1 car. Much of this is dissipated as heat, noise, wear and so on. If you could increase that even to 92 per cent, it would release approximately 15 horsepower and make it available to drive the car faster. The oil may have a valuable role in this and Ferrari is the ideal team to carry out this development as it is unique in having a total engine-car team.

Brawn also had a programme of modifications to the suspension which would improve the handling of the car. 'I'd like to see some feel come back into the steering. I think that the sensitivity of the steering is not very good, which is something that may be hindering Eddie more than Michael. I want to have the steering more direct than it is now. We are working on suspension geometry, part of which is to do with the steering. At the moment the entry to a corner is very critical. We can't do anything about the middle of the corner as the entry becomes even more critical, so you're balancing. We can stop understeer in the middle by having a lot of oversteer on entry, which is not necessarily the best solution. So what we have at the moment is the best compromise between the two. We have a power steering system, which because of its design takes a bit of feel away from the driver. I want to try and bring that back. It's a pretty major package, involving a complete re-design of the front suspension. What we're looking for is a bit more stability on entry, and a bit more consistency between entry and middle.'

To achieve this Brawn was planning a complete scan of the suspension geometry to see what was required. 'We've got a differential programme going on at the moment that we've been working on for six months, but I won't let it go on the car as we haven't finally quantified the advantage of it. We've had it on the car many times and it's progressing the whole time, but when we put it on the car against the differential we have, the gain is either very small or not apparent at all.

'Obviously, people have put a lot of work and effort into it and they want to see it on the car, but I feel if we put it on the car now we might be taking a backward step.'

As Brawn points out when talking about hasty changes made in the name of progress, 'You saw it with McLaren one or two years ago. They were making enormous changes and not getting anywhere. However, if you look at the best example of cautiousness, Williams, you see their changes are very slow and methodical. They do, of course, have the advantage of being the quickest and that always makes life easier.'

However, there were still new things for France and others being planned for Silverstone. 'We've got a front wing here [France] which is very new. We still have to decide whether to race with it or not.'

ANOTHER VICTORY
IT TURNED OUT TO BE A GREAT RACE

For the French Grand Prix, Ferrari did race with the new front wing and it was credited with making an important difference to the handling of the car. After Michael Schumacher expressed his doubts as to whether the Ferrari would do well at the Magny-Cours circuit, against all odds he snatched pole position, while team-mate Eddie Irvine was fifth on the starting grid. It turned out to be a great race for the stable of the prancing horse, as Schumacher went on to obtain his sixth victory for Ferrari, while Irvine was on the podium in third place.

Ross Brawn explained the advantages of the new wing. 'It's more efficient, creating more downforce with less drag. Wings, particularly front wings, are very dynamic. They can affect the cars' feel and its behaviour.' Irvine agreed that the car was now easier to drive and to set up.

The new 046/2 engine was also given the go-ahead at Magny-Cours and was used in the race for the first time. It had been beset by problems, which were solved by Ferrari and Shell. As Brawn says, 'We had a problem with some parts of the 046/2 engine. Paolo Martinelli identified the trouble and we looked at options to resolve it. Shell developed another lubricant which virtually eliminated the problem.'

Ross Brawn is not only a technical man but also an excellent 'manager of people'. His open-minded approach to refusing to place people in boxes is one of the reasons for his success. 'There is a lot of pressure on people who work in Formula One, as well as a high level of skill and talent required. When you put these things together you probably have a situation where people in motor racing are not entirely "normal".

'We're not too worried about people's attitudes as long as they're reasonably positive. We are concerned about their ability and whether they are ultimately making the car go faster. Within reason, if someone has a lot of personality problems, it doesn't matter, as long as it's not upsetting the team. What you have to do wherever you go is learn to adapt to the people around you. I think it is a mistake to go to a team and bring people with you. There may well be more capable people at the new team than you had working with you before. It takes a little time to adjust to everyone's needs at your new team. It took me a few months to understand what people actually meant when they said something.

'However, in terms of the personnel at Ferrari, they're as good as anyone in Formula One. Giorgio [Ascanelli] is an exceptional engineer. Jean [Todt] is an exceptional team director. I look at them and they look at me, and I'm sure I do things differently to what they're used to. But if we can combine all those things without too much conflict we can be successful. Jean takes away a lot of the pressure, he absorbs a lot, but there is only so much he can hold back. The rest you have to take yourself.

'One thing that has changed is that the responsibility is now Maranello's, and nobody else's. We have to solve problems ourselves, whereas in the past when FDD [John Barnard's Ferrari Design and Development, which was based in England] had a different point of view, we could not find a joint solution. Now we have the designer, the chief engineer and the technical director at Maranello. If there's a problem, we have to solve it; there's no bouncing it about like a ping-pong ball.'

This confirms John Barnard's view that in 1996 a lot of the problems were caused by each side − FDD and Maranello − blaming the other, and is a good indicator that the right technical director can bring order and prevent a damaging civil war from breaking out. The new set-up at Maranello would also help people like Giorgio Ascanelli who could now concentrate on engineering. But, strangely enough, Ascanelli was out of sorts and struggling to come to terms with the meaning of it all at Magny-Cours. I made the mistake of calling Nigel Stepney the team co-ordinator rather than chief mechanic, although Stepney, up to this point, had always been referred to as team co-ordinator. Ascanelli put me right. 'He's chief mechanic.' But isn't he more than that, doesn't he pull it all together? 'My dear friend, what has he got to co-ordinate? Mechanics. What do you call the co-ordinator of mechanics? Chief mechanic. He's chief mechanic, full stop.'

In 1996, Ascanelli likened his relationship with Nigel Stepney to a marriage, with each partner learning to work together through talent and compromise. It seemed that the marriage of convenience was a bit frayed around the edges, although it was also obvious that there is a great deal of mutual respect between the two.

Ascanelli, it appeared, was going through a kind of early mid-life crisis. He has a creative mind and comes up with brilliant ideas, but like most creative people he needs space to breathe and a not too controlling master. Irvine says, 'Giorgio is very emotional, very volatile, but he has some great ideas. He's a very clever guy. Sometimes, you've got to listen to him because he's right, other times you just let him have his say and then do what you think is right. Ross is very methodical and will control things. He's less inspired but more organized.'

According to Ascanelli, 'Nigel and I had one kind of relationship in the first two years that we worked together, when I was his only input. At this very minute, I think my role has slightly changed. Now Ross is here so I have a lot less input on design. In Italian I am the *responsabile operativo*, which means that any kind of engineering or mechanical operation comes under my control. Nigel is still strictly responsible to me.'

Reading between the lines, it seemed that Ascanelli was feeling slightly threatened by the changes, although in reality he was still much valued for his creativity and talent. He has more time to spend with his family, wife Stefania and daughter Camilla, but even in that he is controlled. 'In reality we do activities that are good for Stefania and Camilla, because I feel that I cause them so much stress that it's important they enjoy what they do with me, rather than me enjoy what I do with them.'

Time to himself is rare. 'I used to be a decent piano player, I used to read books, now the only time I read is during the race weekend or at tests, as this is the only time I'm alone.

When I'm at home there is always something to do. I don't have the luxury of being alone. I used to be a good amateur photographer and before I broke my leg skiing, I was an awful skier, but a good tennis player and a good volleyball player.'

He wants to retire soon but has no specific dream. 'My father used to tell me, "Live every day of your life as though it was the first or last". I'm trying to do that and be respected. The way you feel and the satisfaction you get depends on what you are and what you bring inside yourself, not what you can do.'

Expanding into the area of philosophy and the meaning of life, he went into Zen mode and declared, 'The secret of being a good archer is not to aim at the target, but to be the target, the archer and the arrow.' He adds, 'I'm probably a bit disillusioned. I've been successful and I'm happy. On the other hand, I believe that if I was to have a much tougher life in a foundry I'd be happier.'

Disillusioned or not, Ferrari was leading both the Drivers' and the Constructors' Championships, and Ascanelli had contributed to the success even if he wasn't doing quite what he wanted to do. However, he expressed his doubts as to whether Ferrari would hang onto its lead in the Constructors' Championship. 'I believe Williams has a technical advantage. We have one advantage over them and he's called Michael Schumacher.'

Meanwhile, Eddie Irvine was still chewing over his qualifying problems and hoping he would overcome them. 'In practice [French Grand Prix Friday session] in the wet, there was nothing between us [him and Schumacher]. In fact, I was even a little bit faster, but there is still this qualifying issue to sort out which I don't understand.

'I used to get out of the Jordan and feel there was nothing left. It wasn't even a good car then, but every other race I would think I'd taken the Jordan to its limit. I was in the top six. The only time I ever did that with the Ferrari was in Australia [his first race in 1996]. Since then never, well, maybe Estoril was close.'

Irvine's race engineer, Luca Baldisserri, has his own theories on the Irishman's qualifying problems. 'There is often only a 100th of a second difference between places in qualifying and I think this makes him nervous. This makes him brake more with his head and less instinctively. When he really tries to go fast, he is slower. It is better when he just does it and it is much more fluid.

'The other aspect that puts pressure on a driver is that it is simpler to overtake when you are higher up the grid. This can also affect your race strategy as you can have a more aggressive strategy if you are ahead – for example, you could have two stops – whereas if you're further down the grid you will try and make one pit stop only.'

Meanwhile at the French Grand Prix at Magny-Cours, Ferrari was celebrating the appearance of both its drivers on the podium. The Italian press were delirious, with one headline reading, 'Ferrari, don't dream, you are World Class'. At last, a win had been achieved that was not dependent on the mistakes of others. Luca di Montezemolo was pleased. 'We were in front from beginning to end, in the dry and in the wet. I don't want to exaggerate, but I think we dominated.'

Schumacher was expressing his surprise at the win. 'My predictions for this race were wrong and this was a convincing win. I hope that at Silverstone we can continue to make good progress as we did here. The race here, which marks the half-way point of the season, will be very important for the Championship.'

Eddie Irvine, having overtaken a couple of cars at the start, finished an impressive third. 'After two bad races I am glad to be back on the podium. Villeneuve braked early so I was able to pass him at the first corner. Towards the end of the race, Villeneuve was closing in on me.'

For Jean Todt it was another confirmation that the team was on the right track. 'We did not expect to have such an advantage in this race, even in wet conditions. We must thank Goodyear for giving us such good tyres. Today was the first time we raced with the 046/2 engine and the decision to use it was not an easy one. The team operated a perfect strategy in a situation that was difficult to judge.'

The cool and calm Schumacher even managed to slow down on the last lap to allow his brother Ralf in the Jordan to go through and complete another lap. Because David Coulthard's McLaren had retired on that lap, it allowed Ralf to pick up one point and was a great birthday present from his big brother.

The Schumacher brothers are very close; when they are both at the same test they are constantly together, usually it is Ralf visiting Michael, but sometimes during race weekend Michael will take refuge in the Jordan motorhome to escape the pressure of people round Ferrari, and have a chat with his little brother. There is no doubt that the elder Schumacher has enormous respect and affection for his younger brother. 'You have to think a long way back to find comparisons with someone who came into Formula One so young and so good without making major mistakes.'

● ● ●

One thing that is certain about motor racing is its unpredictable nature and, sure enough, after the euphoria of the Italian press and the happiness of the team in France, Ferrari was in for a cold shower at the British Grand Prix at Silverstone.

CHAPTER SEVEN

A Cold Shower

'Jean Todt has absolute integrity and also

absolute power when necessary.'

Claudio Berro
Ferrari Chief Press Officer

The Ferrari team touched down at Luton at 9.30 am on the Thursday before the British Grand Prix. Before midday everyone was bustling about the garage unpacking and dressing it in the sponsors' colours. A tape by the Spice Girls and the Italian music cassettes that had been played after the win in France were put to one side. In their place was a heavy beat disco-type sound that reflected their unpacking, or 'getting in the mood' as one mechanic put it.

Occasionally, Jean Todt appeared like an irritated parent and complained about the noise, before taking refuge in the team motorhome and immersing himself in work. In general, though, at the mid-way point of the 1997 season he was looking much more relaxed and at peace with himself than he had at the same time last year, when the team was in the midst of coping with disaster after disaster.

Indeed, Todt was not only surviving but also managing to build the team in the way he wanted. The external and internal pressures of achieving this have been great. It has only been Todt's determination, hard work and vision of the way the team needed to go that have kept things moving in a forward direction. The panic factor, when everything is turned upside down in the face of severe problems, has been eradicated and Todt, with his calm influence, can take most of the credit for that. 'Last year at this same point, it was a nightmare, a disaster. I could not feel happy,' he says.

Despite the disasters, Todt generally doesn't suffer sleepless nights over his professional life. 'Most of the time I sleep well, which is probably why I'm still here. I don't panic. Business is business. It's a part of life, but it's not vital. You have to be pragmatic. If you are affected by something close to you then you are not pragmatic – you are just reacting with your heart. In business you must react with your head.'

Reacting with his head means that he is separated from his family, who live in France, for much of the time. 'I work in Italy and most of the time I'm alone. It's part of the deal and I have to accept it. Anyway, the Italian people who I meet in restaurants and so on are very nice. It's too difficult for someone to be with me while I'm working 16 hours a day in the middle of nowhere. When I go home to Paris for the weekend I go to my other life, but I can never be completely unplugged from business. I couldn't go two days without knowing what is happening.'

After four tough years things were finally coming together. 'From an organizational point of view, we [Ferrari] have almost achieved what we wanted to achieve. It's taken four years to bring things together, find the right people and put them in the right places. Out of 100 people (including engine, chassis, production, composite, foundry and administration staff) we still need a software expert, two chassis designers and a composite designer. Once we've found them, then there will be the normal turnover of staff, so we will always be looking for new people.'

It is clear that there is mutual respect and admiration between Todt and Ross Brawn. Brawn's arrival at the stable has also given Todt a partner. 'Ross is a great guy, very professional and very level-headed. He's achieving what he was brought in to do.'

Todt is not a person to celebrate wildly when Ferrari wins a race. He is always aware of the consequences that such an action could bring. 'I'm not the kind of person to jump on the table and show how happy I am, because first and foremost I am always concerned about the next race. I just think we must have a silent and [pause as he searches for the right word] humble approach, otherwise the boomerang comes and lands on the back of your head very quickly. I am always scared it will come back.'

Silverstone was the right place to be cautious. 'When we say we're reliable, it's difficult to get the words out as I think that maybe tomorrow we won't be reliable.' Quite. The first indication that things wouldn't go to plan at Silverstone was when Eddie Irvine collided with a hare in qualifying. The collision not only scared the hell out of him, it also meant that the car needed a new nose cone and turning vane. Despite that, he pulled himself together and qualified seventh, three places behind Schumacher, who said, 'I hope I can make it onto the podium on race day.' Unfortunately for Schumacher, it wasn't to be. He took control of the race when Jacques Villeneuve had to endure a 33-second pit stop after a wheel nut jammed. Then, having built up a big lead, the German's left rear wheel bearing failed, putting him out of the race with 20 laps to go.

Ten minutes later, Eddie Irvine experienced the second mechanical failure when his right half shaft failed as he was pulling away from his pit stop. *Nil points* for Ferrari.

Despite the disappointment, Schumacher was trying to be positive about the situation. 'It would have been better if I could have finished the race, but these things happen. We had confirmation of another important aspect, the fact that we are now competitive during the race. When I retired from the race, I was leading it by a good margin. We have to improve our qualifying performance, but I'm sure we will resolve our problems before the next Grand Prix in Germany.'

Behind the scenes a much worse disaster – at least in the eyes of the paddock gourmets – had occurred. The team cook, Claudio Degli Espositi, had been taken ill with a fever forcing him to stay in bed on the Saturday. He struggled to the paddock on race day, but was still pale and under the weather. In Italy everything revolves around the kitchen, so Salvatore from the Philip Morris motorhome was drafted in to help Bruno Romani keep the team fed and happy.

In terms of the race, it was sad to see Ignazio Lunetta walking back disconsolately into the garage from the pit wall clutching his laptop computer, but the atmosphere was not too depressed. Schumacher was still leading lead the Drivers' Championship by four points and Ferrari was top of the Constructors' Championship with a three-point lead over Williams. As Nigel Stepney said, 'We just have to get ourselves together.'

THE MEDIA AT WORK
THE ITALIAN PRESS WERE KEEPING CALM

The desire to be anonymous was reaching epic proportions for Eddie Irvine. He is undoubtedly a complex character – a lad who likes the women and the night life, but hates people staring at him; an ambitious racing driver who wants to be Number One for one of the top teams but hates his loss of privacy. As the Irishman says: 'It's very important for a racing driver to be the centre of attention. You have to feel that the whole team is behind you and relying on you. Michael has that. I'd like to be Number One at Ferrari or any of the top teams. At Benetton you can see the input a driver can have. They've achieved little since Michael left, and yet they have a better car now than they've ever had before.'

Not that Irvine is unhappy with his lot. Racing has brought many material benefits. 'The amount of money you make at the race track gives you a good lifestyle away from it. I've got a house bought and paid for. All my toys are paid for. I don't owe anybody anything. I don't owe the bank anything. To have that independence and control is quite nice.'

Michael Schumacher's wife Corinna had been at Silverstone to watch the British Grand Prix. Corinna is as unaffected, natural and friendly as she was when she and Michael first met. What seems to keep their feet on the ground is a love of the simple things in life. Neither of them is a big city sophisticate. They prefer a country life with dogs and children and long walks. Corinna keeps out of the limelight and lets Michael get on with his job.

Unlike some of the drivers' wives and girlfriends who pirouette and preen about the paddock as though they were the stars, Corinna takes a more low profile approach. Despite this, there is a price to be paid for being the wife of a double World Champion, and the television cameras and photographers are never far away.

Although Michael says he finds it difficult to talk about himself, it is clear he finds peace and tranquillity with his growing family in the relative quiet of his country home near Lake Geneva in Switzerland.

Following Silverstone, the Italian press were keeping admirably calm instead of screaming for someone's head. This most unusual situation could be attributed in part to the fact that Ferrari was thus far having a good season and in part to Claudio Berro, Ferrari's chief press officer. Level-headed and with a balanced temperament, Berro is always organized and very methodical in his approach, and for the first time, Ferrari was noticeably relaxed in its approach to the media, who were encouraged to drop in for coffee or lunch, with well-researched articles always noted and the writer contacted and thanked.

Berro is always on the go. He's a workaholic who knows how to deal with the team and the media in a way that will keep everyone happy. Ring him at 7 am and he's arriving at the office, ring him at 10 pm and he's just finishing his round-up of what the Italian media are up to.

One of the most popular Berro initiatives is the instigation of a very useful media booklet. Not only does this booklet give pertinent information about each race track – including previous races, quotes about the circuit from Jean Todt and the drivers, dates and times of practice, qualifying, the race and the press conferences – it also gives a summary of the season's other races, and has blank pages for recording information and writing down interviews.

During the week leading up to a race weekend the media pressure builds in intensity. The usual 25 to 30 pages of press cuttings turn into 60 or 70 on the Wednesday and Thursday before a race, 120 on the Friday and Saturday, and 150 on race day. The day after race day, they peak at 200.

Each day, Berro receives anything up to a dozen faxes requesting interviews from all over the world. In addition, television stations want access to Fiorano on test days and have to be monitored and given help.

At the races the planned interviews have to be monitored and organized. The drivers and all the team personnel involved in the FIA official press conferences have to be escorted to the venue of the press conference and then escorted back through the mêlée (in Schumacher's case) of radio and television reporters, and journalists.

Race day is almost peaceful in comparison, according to Berro. 'It's quite calm after the previous run-around. I receive the press cuttings between 7.15 and 7.30 in the morning. One set comes to me, one set to Jean Todt, and two sets for the journalists. While reading my copy, I eat a ham sandwich and some fruit. Then we have warm-up. I'm always in the garage to make notes of everything: the cars used, the tyres used, and

A QUESTION OF FUEL

Using sophisticated analysis equipment, fuel company Shell helps Ferrari to monitor its fuel and lubricants. Simon Dunning is one of Shell's men at the track side. He explains: 'The formulation of F1 fuel is achieved in the same way as for the fuel you buy for your car. In the past, we added hydrocarbon materials to the petrol to enhance performance, but the FIA consulted the fuel companies and asked us to produce fuel that was basically the same as that used in road cars – even though the combination might be different. Formula One is like a thoroughbred horse. You may have different trainers but broadly speaking the experience and type of your horse affects your decisions, and you adapt the fuel to suit.

'Unlike a road car, we don't have to make fuel to cope with cold weather conditions, or a lot of start–stop situations. Our major concern is to extract maximum power. A modern F1 car will do about four miles to the gallon, although fuel consumption is an issue only where consumption makes the difference between two and three pit stops. However, our in-depth research helps to improve the fuel that you use in your road car. Shell has an expert in-house who can tell what difference the various fuels make to a racing car, even if it is one that isn't in the same class as the Ferrari Formula One car. In F1, fuel regulations are very tight. You always have to submit a sample of any new fuel to FIA, and once it is approved you make it up into big enough quantities usually to supply two races. Every time we make up a new batch we submit it for approval.'

the time the drivers leave and return to the garage. If a journalist asks me for the information and it's not secret, I can then tell him. If, on the other hand, a journalist makes a mistake I have the information to correct him.

THE BATTLEFIELD
OBSERVING THE CALM BEFORE THE STORM

Formula One is like a battle and Todt effectively goes into battle at every race. Like most clever men, he often feels the cold blast of insecurity, and Berro is his security blanket. 'You have to know him to appreciate him. He can appear to be hard and rigid if you don't know him. But when he shakes his hand and gives his word, it is the same as a written contract. He has absolute integrity and also absolute power when necessary. Everyone responds to his orders. When he has time he will listen to everyone, but when the moment arrives to take a decision he always takes it.'

Before a race, Berro walks around observing other teams. It is, as he puts it, 'the calm before the storm'. He also has great technical ability. In the past when other teams saw the Ferrari press officer strolling around the cars they didn't take much notice – that was until they discovered that Berro had studied engineering. Now when Williams personnel, for example, see him approaching them on the starting grid they form a human barrier round the car!

During a race Berro is in the garage with all the other members of the team to observe the pit stops of both Ferraris and the other competing teams. After the race there is always a flurry of activity. The press release has to be written and printed, and Berro also assists Todt and/or the drivers in their post-race interviews. After that, faxes are sent to the sponsors, a document of information on the Grand Prix is prepared, and an internal press release (which is highly confidential and for team members only) is written.

Like most of his colleagues, Berro believes Ferrari is more together this year. 'We are more of a team. It's more complete now that we have a technical director who works at Maranello. The exchange of information is more immediate. All the meetings are at Maranello and the car is built in one place, so no one can blame anyone else.'

● ● ●

Next stop for the millionaire boys with their flash toys was Hockenheim – and a home race for Michael Schumacher. Now we would see if Ferrari's challenge for the World Championship was serious or just a flash in the pan.

CHAPTER EIGHT

The Fight Back

'I've been involved in the sport too long

not to know that until you pass the

chequered flag anything can happen.'

Jean Todt
Ferrari Team Director

Although Ferrari and Williams were the only teams with a serious chance of winning the World Championship in 1997, the German Grand Prix was all about Benetton and the comeback of old-timer Gerhard Berger. The Austrian driver had been absent through the recurrence of a sinus problem for the previous three races, and had also suffered the devastating loss of his father in a plane crash.

Fellow Austrian Alexander Wurz had shown he was a worthy replacement. So at Hockenheim Berger had everything to prove — and he did it in style: pole position and race winner. It was Benetton's first victory since 1995. Michael Schumacher was the first to congratulate the experienced Berger. 'He drove a great race,' said the Ferrari Number One.

Berger had pulled away from the chasing pack right at the start of the race, and by lap 5 he had extended his lead by half a lap. The young Italian Giancarlo Fisichella, racing for the Jordan team, was lying second with seven laps remaining when he had to retire due to a tyre puncture. Schumacher took advantage of this to move up from third. However, five laps from the end of the race the Ferrari team had to call the German into the pits for an unprogrammed 'splash and dash' fuel top up. Fortunately, Schumacher rejoined the race still ahead of third-placed Hakkinen, and managed to pull away from the Finn to finish second.

It turned out that the Ferrari team's planned one-stop strategy had to be altered for Schumacher when insufficient fuel was put into the tank. This wasn't the only problem. The gears had been playing up during the last 30 laps, with the result that Schumacher couldn't engage fifth. Meanwhile, trouble with the rear wing meant that the Ferrari was losing a certain amount of grip. Ross Brawn explains: 'When fifth gear became reluctant to engage we were losing out slightly on straight-line speed. In addition a small flap on the rear wing disappeared, so Michael started to get oversteer. He thought it was the tyres, but when we lost the flap he gained one or two kilometres in a straight line. We could see what was happening on the telemetry from about lap 16.'

In the end, though, second place for Schumacher meant six points, keeping him ahead of rival Jacques Villeneuve by 10 points. The Canadian didn't finish the race, having gone off under pressure from Jarno Trulli (who was driving the Prost car in place of the recovering Olivier Panis). As usual Schumacher was low-key. 'There's work to do and we'll get down to it immediately, even if we're still leading the Championship.'

This wasn't the first time in the season that a Ferrari had needed a 'splash and dash'. In Melbourne a similar thing had happened. Pino D'Agostino, who is in charge of the engine and the fuel at the track explains: 'All the teams occasionally experience this problem. It occurs because the fuel tank is divided into several cells, to make sure the weight distribution of the car is even. This can lead to regurgitation of the fuel into the hose when one cell is full. By monitoring the amount of fuel that has gone into the cells we should know when some has been left out.' At Hockenheim 10kg by weight was left out – enough to mean that Schumacher didn't have sufficient fuel in his tank to make it to the end of the race.

Schumacher declared after Hockenheim: 'I will try and win the World Championship, but I don't want to succeed because an adversary [presumably Villeneuve] goes off the track. I like to battle and beat my rivals during the race.'

Team-mate Eddie Irvine, on the other hand, did not have a happy race. Still beset by qualifying problems, he nevertheless managed to move from 10th place, where he had qualified, to fifth place at the start of the race, only to be struck from behind by Villeneuve's team-mate, Heinz-Harald Frentzen, thus ending the Irishman's race ended before it had properly begun.

Irvine's race engineer, the faithful Luca Baldisserri, had his own idea about why it had gone wrong in qualifying. 'Before Hockenheim all the other drivers tested at Monza, which is a similar low downforce circuit. Eddie tested at Fiorano, so we arrived in Germany with a disadvantage. Eddie is improving in qualifying, but he still finds it difficult to unblock himself and give the maximum on a qualifying lap.'

Giorgio Ascanelli, who now had overall control of Eddie's car, sees things in a similar light. 'Eddie overdrives the car. These cars are extremely sensitive; you can't "hassle" them. They're light, they act strangely when you overdrive and as a result you feel as if you're going to slide all the time. Michael is smooth because he lets the car have its head. Eddie is much quicker when he thinks he hasn't tried. He is much better in the race when he's alone in the car and not listening to anyone on the radio. He can get distracted – and as a driver you must have 100 per cent concentration. Having said this, for anyone to be compared to Michael Schumacher is very difficult. Eddie is without doubt as good as any of the other drivers after Michael.'

Ascanelli regarded Hockenheim as an opportunity missed although he admitted, 'Having said it was a lost chance, Williams had a dreadful race and again that helped us. We made mistakes, but Williams made bigger mistakes.'

It had been a tense week for Eddie, whose contract ran out on the 31 July. For some time there had been speculation in the press that either one of the Finns, Salo or Hakkinen, would be chosen for the Ferrari Number Two hot seat. But it all ended happily for Eddie when he was reconfirmed as Schumacher's team-mate for 1998.

THE PROBLEM OF TYRES
THEY WERE WEARING OUT BEFORE HIS EYES

For the next Grand Prix a fortnight later at the tight and twisty Hungaroring (in Hungary), Ferrari was looking forward to putting more distance between itself and Williams in the Constructors' Championship. Williams, however, was desperate to close the gap on its rivals and forget the misfortunes of Hockenheim.

Things began brightly for the team as Schumacher qualified brilliantly on pole and Irvine was fifth. However, during race day warm-up, despite a reconfigured F310B equipped with a Step 1 V10 engine instead of the Step 2, Michael Schumacher crashed the lighter chassis car and was forced to drive the spare. This resulted in bad tyre wear and three pit stops rather than the planned two.

Having led on the first lap, Schumacher soon discovered that the team had chosen the wrong tyres. He had to stop first on lap 14, then twice more during the race. In one of the best races of the year so far, Damon Hill, in his Arrows, had been leading for some time before clutch problems forced him to slow down, allowing Villeneuve to overtake the hapless 1996 World Champion on the last lap.

Meanwhile, Schumacher was staggering round on tyres that were almost wearing out before his very eyes. He was helped by brother Ralf (which went down like a lead balloon in the Jordan camp) and by team-mate Irvine, who protected the Championship leader by forming a barrier behind him, enabling

Schumacher to cross the line in fourth place. Eddie Irvine, meanwhile, was having a torrid time. He had been shunted out of the race by the Prost of Shinji Nakano when in sixth place with only one lap to go. With his exit, one valuable point for his team disappeared into thin air.

So Ferrari left the Hungaroring with Schumacher still leading the Drivers' Championship by just three points and with the team leading the Constructors' Championship by a margin of two. Jean Todt was resigned to the results of the race. 'I've been involved in the sport too long not to know that until you pass the chequered flag anything can happen.'

Giorgio Ascanelli felt that the Grand Prix at Hungary was one race where perhaps Williams had outfoxed the rest. 'I don't think Hungary was down to luck. I think Villeneuve was clever. We knew the tyres were going to blister as soon as we started pushing. It's a difficult circuit to overtake on, so I felt that we should have taken it easy. Damon [Hill] was pushing, but he wasn't in contention for the World Drivers' Championship so maybe we should have let him go and saved our tyres. We knew the first six laps would be critical and Michael did his best time on the first lap. I'm not saying the drivers are stupid, I'm saying the team wasn't strong enough in taking into account the tyres. We briefed the drivers on tyres, but maybe we weren't as decisive as we should have been.'

Schumacher, however, had been aware of the need to save his tyres. 'We had serious tyre problems from the first lap, just like at Barcelona. During the first few laps I tried to go slower to conserve them as much as possible, but it was useless.'

According to Ignazio Lunetta, 'We seem to stress the tyres more because of the way the drivers drive and also because of the characteristics of the car, compared to either Williams or Benetton.'

STILL FIGHTING
THE BATTLE WASN'T OVER YET

After Hungary, Jean Todt was in fighting mood. Known as the Napoleon of the pit lane, Todt is not one to give up easily. 'The battle will be long but we will defend ourselves by working even harder. At least for now, it's the others that have to follow us.'

Schumacher may be cautious by nature, but he is not one to give up either. 'I always look to the future with optimism and as the next race is Spa, my favourite circuit, there is a good chance of success. I am a little more worried about Monza. We didn't go very well at Monza during the last test session, but we are testing there from tomorrow so we'll try and improve the situation.'

Next stop: the Spa-Francorchamps circuit in Belgium. According to Lunetta, 'We always travel happily to Spa. It's a beautiful circuit for drivers, with the formidable Eau Rouge and Blanchimont corners. You always have to be aware of the weather, of course, as it is so unpredictable. It is a constant challenge to keep one eye on the skies and the other on the competing teams.'

In Schumacher's case, it is usually a case of the other teams keeping an eye on him. Spa 1997 turned out to be as good as Spa 1996 for the German. Before the race, he had taken the precaution of preparing both the race car and the T-car with different set-ups. Some 20 minutes prior to the start, the heavens opened. He made the crucial decision to go for the intermediate set-up on the T-car, while both the Williams and Benetton on the grid in front of him were on full wet.

Schumacher's gamble worked perfectly, particularly as the

race began behind the Safety Car, expertly driven by Oliver Gavin (former British Formula Three champion and a regular behind the wheel of the Safety Car), until the start of lap 4. Then it was the Michael Schumacher show, and the crowd watched in awe as he roared round the circuit lap after lap, demonstrating his skill.

Some teams complained about the presence of the Safety Car and said that had they known they would be starting behind it, they would have changed their set-up and strategy. Lunetta is dismissive of the whingers. 'The rules are clear. If the Safety Car is there at the five-minute board, then it will start the race. If it's not there, then the start is regular. It's clear for all to see.'

PERFECT STATEGY
THE WEATHER GODS MUST BE SCHUMACHER FANS

You would have thought that people would have learnt from Schumacher's supreme performance in the rain at Monaco earlier in the year. As he says, 'My race car, with the lightweight chassis, was set up for the dry, and the T-car for mixed conditions, with less fuel on board, because of the possibility of having to make an early stop for slicks. When the pit lane opened, I ran one lap in the race car and then decided to go with the spare.

'Most people were on wets, but I decided to go with the intermediates. They had worked for me at Monaco, and I thought it was worth gambling on the fact that it was a heavy shower and wouldn't last long.' As the heavens opened Ross Brawn smiled. 'I think the weather gods may be Michael Schumacher fans!'

Giorgio Ascanelli explains, 'With a bit of cunning we waited until the last minute to send the cars out on the track;

COOKING FOR AN ARMY

As Prince Albert of Monaco will be the first to admit, the food provided by Ferrari during race weekends is always delicious. And this is down to two men.

In charge of the team motorhome are cooks Bruno Romani and Claudio Degli Espositi. And their combined effort is greatly appreciated not only by the 50 or so team members that attend each of the races and who require feeding on a regular basis, but also by the many guests that Ferrari entertains during the course of a race weekend.

In order to meet their own high culinary standards, Romani and Espositi endure many hours of hard work. The cooks arrive at the circuit at 6.30 or 7 in the morning and leave at 11 or 11.30 at night.

The salami, proscuitto, mortadella, Parmesan cheese, pasta, olive oil and balsamic vinegar that are the essence of Italian cooking are all brought from Italy. The fresh vegetables are brought in locally. At each Grand Prix the team consumes enough to keep an army on the go, as the following list shows.

10–12 bottles of olive oil
40kg of pasta
10–12kg of Parmesan cheese
20kg of proscuitto
7kg of salami
8kg of mortadella
45kg of vegetables
25kg of meat
150 litres of mineral water (a mixture of still and carbonated)
40 bottles of wine

THE FERRARI MECHANICS

Some 34 mechanics travel with the team, excluding the two race engineers. It's not a job for the faint-hearted. It is rare to arrive at the circuit after seven in the morning and leave before eight or nine at night. A problem in practice can keep them there until the early hours of the morning or one night can run into the next day with no sleep taken. Combine that with the constant travel and changing climates and the job needs 100 per cent commitment.

we know it can rain here as it's done so many times in the last 10 years. [In fact, it had rained at Spa at some point during the previous 11 Grand Prix weekends, and would do so again with dramatic consequences at the 1998 Grand Prix.] We sent the cars out in the rain to give them a feel of what the circuit was like. One driver made a choice that was conservative, and one made the aggressive choice and won.'

It took Schumacher a mere two laps of the race proper to pass Villeneuve and Alesi as though they were just incidentals to the main party, and establish a lead of six seconds. By the next lap this lead had increased to 17 seconds, and at the end of the race, he was more than 26 seconds faster than the second-placed Villeneuve. It was yet another driving masterpiece by the German.

Unfortunately for team-mate Eddie Irvine, Spa was an instantly forgettable race as he tangled with Pedro Diniz's Arrows on the last lap.

Luca Baldisserri explains, 'Spa was the only race this year where Eddie and his team really got it wrong. A true disaster. The car went quite well in the wet but Eddie only had two complete laps on Saturday in free practice and qualifying. We had only one complete lap in qualifying due to a series of problems. In the race we chose the wrong tyres. It was wet, but we could have chosen intermediates.'

But if Michael Schumacher, the grand rain master, chose intermediates, then why didn't Eddie follow his example? 'We were further down the grid,' Baldisserri explained. What about the radio? 'We try not to discuss strategic decisions on the radio as the other teams can hear us.'

NEXT STOP, MONZA
THE *TIFOSI* WERE BAYING FOR SUCCESS

Schumacher left Spa 12 points ahead of Jacques Villeneuve in the Drivers' Championship while Ferrari was eight points ahead in the Constructors' Championship. Next race was Monza, where the *tifosi* would be baying for a repeat of the consecutive Spa/Monza victories of 1996.

However, before the race there was testing. The pressure was building as Fiat Boss Gianni Agnelli graced the test session with his presence on the Wednesday. Accompanying him was Ferrari Chairman Luca di Montezemolo. Both men were relaxed and optimistic. Sitting at the top of the Drivers' Championship and the Constructors' Championship is a good vantage point from which to view the world. As Ross Brawn says, 'If the fans look back to where we were in January and February, I think they would have snapped your hand off if you'd asked them "Do you want four victories by September?"'

Meanwhile Michael Schumacher and Eddie Irvine were hard at work. One of the most pressing problems was getting the aerodynamic set-up on the car just right for the fast Monza circuit. It would be tight, but there were still 10 days. For

Ferrari, Monza is the circuit where there is the most pressure. The eyes of the world are on the Scuderia, including Fiat, the media, the *tifosi*, and the celebrities and VIP guests of the sponsors. It's four days of constant chaos.

Montezemolo would be watching the race at home, as he always does. 'I'm very nervous when I watch Monza. I want to be on my own. I don't want to feel under any obligation. I want to be free to express my reactions, either positive or negative. I don't want anyone to distract me by asking questions.'

Except, that is, Agnelli who also admits, 'I often call Luca during the races to get information which he has at his fingertips. I always find him very nervous and agitated ... and, in truth, I have to say that I have my heart in my mouth during the races.'

● ● ●

With the way things turned out at the team's home Grand Prix in Italy, there would be good reason for this state of anxiety.

CHAPTER NINE

September Doldrums

'The challenge of designing a car for Ferrari was enough to persuade me to come out of retirement.'

Rory Byrne
Ferrari Chief Designer 1997

All the attention was now focused on Monza and the Italian Grand Prix. On the Friday during free practice the Ferrari team had been working hard in preparation for race day. As Jean Todt says, 'On Friday it was difficult to get a clear picture of our car's performance as some of the cars' times had been set on new tyres and, furthermore, we did not know how much fuel the other cars had in their tanks.'

By the end of the qualifying session on Saturday, they did have a clearer picture – and it wasn't good. Michael Schumacher ended up in ninth place, his worst qualifying position of the season, while Eddie Irvine was 10th. Ross Brawn commented, 'Last year Michael was a second off pole position and third on the grid. This year he is 6/10ths of a second off pole and he's ninth.'

Ferrari was convinced that there was not much more that could be done in developing the 1997 car. Brawn declares, 'We've got to the stage where there's nothing left to do on the basic car. We've had new wings, new floors, a different chassis and suspension; in fact we've done everything without re-designing the car completely.'

One of the principle new designs has been the lightweight chassis. Brawn says, 'I looked at ways of saving weight together with Rory Byrne (the new chief designer). The major advantage of having a lighter chassis is that we can put all the weight on the floor of the car and lower the centre of gravity. This means the car will corner faster and brake better. At the same time, we took advantage of the fact we were creating a new chassis to increase the car's fuel capacity.

'At Melbourne our race strategy was compromised because we couldn't put any more fuel in the car. It looked likely that Monza was going to be a race where fuel capacity would be important. In fact it was, and we were able to stay out one lap

A TRUE FAN...
Ninety-year-old Silvio Ferri, a lifelong Ferrari devotee, enjoying the fruits of victory at Monza in 1996.

MEN AT WORK...
The Ferrari mechanics busy in the team garage, where they are making the necessary fine-tuning to Schumacher's car before another practice session.

A QUESTION OF TRUST...
Michael Schumacher with his race engineer Ignazio Lunetta, the man who looks after his driver's interests at the race track and ensures the car is set up exactly as the German wants it.

ALL IN THE FAMILY...
Eddie Irvine, sister Sonia, and parents Edmund and Kathleen gather for a family conference.

SLICK STRATEGY... Suzuka 97 witnessed a true team performance from the Ferrari drivers, with both securing a podium position.

GERMAN GRIEF... Schumacher on the way to a collision with Jacques Villeneuve, which finally extinguished the German's bid for the 1997 World Drivers' Championship.

A STUDY IN CONCENTRATION...
Jean Todt, Ignazio Lunetta and Pino D'Agostino preparing for Brazil 98.

NEW SEASON, NEW HOPES...
Irvine in the T-car finishes fourth as Ferrari make a stuttering start to the 1998 season in Australia.

VICTORY AT LAST!...
Schumacher takes the chequered flag (above) to win the 1998 Argentinian Grand Prix, and celebrates (left) with a delighted Jean Todt and Eddie Irvine, who finished third.

CANADA 98...
Despite a collision with Heinz-Harald Frentzen, Schumacher (top) and Ferrari celebrated a one-three podium finish – this after the race was restarted twice.

'WHAT CAN I SAY?'...
A dramatic 1998 British Grand Prix at Silverstone saw Schumacher win a rain-drenched race after having to come into the pits for a stop-go penalty on the last lap.

SECOND TIME ROUND...
Schumacher and Irvine lead the two McLarens at the second start of the 1998 French Grand Prix at Magny-Cours, in what proved to be a one-two finish for Ferrari.

BIG IN BUDAPEST...
Schumacher's fifth win of the season in Hungary (left) brought him ever-closer to Mika Hakkinen at the top of the 1998 World Drivers' Championship. Ferrari and Shell personnel know how to have a celebration (below).

A SOAKING AT SPA...
A disastrous race for the Scuderia, with Schumacher retiring after a controversial collision with Coulthard, and Irvine going off into a gravel trap.

MEETING THE SPONSORS...
Jean Todt discusses some technical details with Tommy Hilfiger.

RELAX BOYS...
Eddie Irvine shares a joke with the Ferrari technical director.

600 AND COUNTING...
Ferrari drivers past and present line up with Chairman Luca di Montezemolo at Monza in September 1998 to celebrate the team's 600th Grand Prix.

HEADING FOR THE CLIMAX...
After their first and second places at the Nurburgring, it's all square between Schumacher and Hakkinen going into the final race of 1998.

TO THE BACK STALLS...
Disaster strikes Schumacher at the final showdown in Japan. His Ferrari stalls at the front of the grid, resulting in a yellow flag and a race restart for the German, this time at the very back.

OVER AND OUT...
Despite a brave recovery drive from the back of the grid to third place, a right rear tyre puncture on lap 32 spelt the end of Schumacher and Ferrari's 1998 championship hopes.

longer than Berger who was challenging Michael during the race, as a result of which we kept Michael in front of him. It was a lot of work but it was worthwhile as it gained us a point – and that might be crucial at the end of the year.

'It's obvious that a 600kg car is faster than a 640kg car. However, if you have two cars that each weigh 640kg then the one with a lower centre of gravity, with all other things being equal, will be faster. That is basic mechanics.'

So what was the problem at Monza? Ignazio Lunetta had a few observations. 'At high-speed circuits we reduce the wing and the car loses a lot of aerodynamics, and the speed doesn't increase by as much as it should do. The car is then not very efficient.'

So at the end of a disappointing Italian Grand Prix for Ferrari, Michael Schumacher finished sixth with Eddie Irvine a further two places behind. As Giorgio Ascanelli said, 'We're eight or nine kilometres an hour slower than most and you can't win Monza like this.'

But it could have been worse for Schumacher and Ferrari. Jacques Villeneuve finished in fifth place, so he only made up one point on Schumacher, leaving the German 10 points ahead in the Drivers' Championship, and Ferrari a perilous one point ahead of Williams in the Constructors' Championship. Lunetta thought Williams had acted strangely. 'If you are in Villeneuve's position, you have to attack. Michael has only to defend. Yet Williams made the first pit stop – this is a defensive move.'

Ascanelli seemed happy enough. 'I am content about the result as I wasn't expecting anything better. Frankly, Villeneuve finishing fifth and Michael sixth was a blessing. If Villeneuve had won the race and Michael had come second with a final sprint, everyone would have said, "Fantastic, the performance is there" and so on. But we would have lost four points to Villeneuve instead of just one.'

Monza, of course, is all about the *tifosi* and they were out in force with their painted faces, waving their Ferrari flags and banners, and hoping for a repeat of the 1996 victory. They were to be disappointed. However, with a World Championship still possible all was not lost. The fans had waited 18 years for a champion driver, and weren't going to give up until the end.

TEAM SPIRIT
THERE WAS STILL AN AIR OF OPTIMISM

After Monza there was still an air of optimism around the Ferrari factory at Fiorano. According to Ross Brawn, 'Michael's in a pretty good frame of mind. He's had a hard period. He had five days' testing at Monza to try and find a better solution with the car, which we didn't really achieve. Then there were the three days of the race itself. If you include the previous race at Spa, he's done a lot of driving. It was frustrating for him at Monza as it was the first race in quite a while that he knew would be difficult to win. At this stage we can't afford an off weekend with Michael.'

Brawn had clearly settled in as technical director and was taking control, and this was having an effect on Giorgio Ascanelli. Whereas Ascanelli was stressed in France, he was calm and philosophical after Monza. 'I feel that my job, as it was, is finishing. Ross is more confident, and more familiar with every aspect of the team, and he's learning Italian. A technical director who is in place and goes to the races doesn't need someone to be in charge of engineering.'

What of the future? 'I don't know what's going to happen,' said Ascanelli. 'I don't want to leave. Ross and I will have to decide what we're going to do with ourselves.' For his part, Brawn was adamant that he wanted Ascanelli by his side. 'You need the capacity to solve problems when they occur, and that means having two or three valued opinions on what needs to be done. I value the input of Giorgio, Rory and the others even though at the end of the day I make the decisions. But it isn't a one-man show.'

Brawn was also mulling over the pressure of Schumacher being in the running for the 1997 Drivers' Championship. 'There will be an enormous amount of disappointment if Michael doesn't win this year. But this should be balanced against the fact that we've won more races than last year. We've built up a good team at Maranello. We've made a lot of progress with a car that looked quite difficult at the beginning of the season. I think the team should be congratulated for its achievements this year. If we should be unfortunate and fail, I don't want people to say that Ferrari threw it away. The truth of the matter is, we weren't expecting to be in this position anyway.'

Add to that Michael Schumacher, who's brilliance covers up the true situation. As Brawn says, 'In some ways the barometer of the car's performance should be judged by Eddie. He's as good as any driver after Michael and you can see the car has only been competitive at three or four circuits: Argentina, San Marino, Monaco and Magny-Cours for example. Michael can mask the situation as he's such a good driver. I think, touch wood (as I don't want to tempt providence), that when we're given half a chance Michael will take it. Spa was a case in point, whereas Silverstone was an example of where we were running strongly before we blew it through mechanical failure. Championships are won over the season, not on the results of a few races.'

After Monza, Nigel Stepney was also feeling the cold wind of failure. 'It was a disappointing result but Villeneuve was only one point ahead of us. I'm satisfied as both cars finished and the team did the best it could. Maybe we didn't go down some of the routes we should have, but it's easy to look back after the event. To be 12 seconds behind the leader in sixth place is unusual in Formula One.

'I think we made very good progress very early on in the season, and we were finishing races and coming up with good strategies when other teams weren't. But the rest have caught up since then. Monza and Hockenheim, for example, weren't strong circuits for us. I think we've lost a bit of our competitiveness.'

PLANNING AHEAD
THE BEST WILL ALWAYS SHINE THROUGH

The year 1997 had certainly been quieter year for Mario Almondo, the man who is head of the production and quality control department. In 1996 there had been constant reliability problems and Almondo was under enormous pressure. So far this year things had been much better. Almondo explains, 'The best part of the job is to construct and develop a new car every year. The production department is involved in everything. If we have too much to do, we have alternative suppliers to make sure reliability is high.'

Meanwhile, Ross Brawn was looking ahead to 1998. 'If we can produce a car that's competitive from Day One and which performs well, then we can concentrate on developing it further, rather than having to recover the situation. I think next year will be the year we can be judged on, as it will be our own car produced at Maranello.'

The new regulations would mean that, in theory, less competitive teams would have a chance to catch up. However, Brawn feels that the best will always shine through. 'A lot of the success of teams is down to the way they work. Those that know how to test, develop and design will be successful. Sometimes, when the rules change a team comes out with a radical approach. For a year the others may be behind, but normally those who do a good job catch up. Next year [1998] Williams and McLaren will be competitive, and so will we.'

With the departure of FDD from the Ferrari equation, the design and development of the entire car had passed back to Maranello. With the loss of the wind tunnel facilities at Bristol, a new wind tunnel was being built by the factory at Fiorano. The man in charge of aerodynamics is Australian Willem Toet. A lively, dapper dresser, he was at Maranello between December 1994 and the autumn of 1998.

These days aerodynamics is more a space science than a terrestrial activity and it's no different at Ferrari. There are five aeronautical engineers working with Toet, each one with his or her own area of responsibility. Toet explains his philosophy on aerodynamics: 'We look at the basic car and isolate the areas that we want to concentrate on. For example, we examine the parts that will be affected by the change in regulations or the fact that they were sensitive in last year's car. We look at how much damage has been caused by a certain aerodynamic factor.

'We design the initial car allowing for certain areas to be modified – for example, the space for the driver's feet. We can still play with the length depending on the height of the driver. We have a preliminary fitting in a mock-up car, which should eliminate most problems, and then we do another final fitting. We try and make the car as aerodynamically perfect as possible, while also allowing for driver comfort.'

In 1998, however, things would change. 'Next year we will not only have a mechanical penalty but also an aerodynamic penalty. We started looking at the 1998 car in March 1997 and we had a 25 per cent loss in downforce, which we believe will translate to a 10 per cent loss once we finish the optimization process. We would lose mechanically even if the tyres weren't grooved, as the car is narrower. I think the best teams have the most to lose.'

The new Ferrari wind tunnel is as impressive artistically as it is technically. Conceived by Renzo Piano, it would form a stunning architectural masterpiece. However, the pragmatic Giorgio Ascanelli declared, 'It's a stylish piece of work — although I would have preferred it to be less flashy and ready earlier.'

Once finished, it would be one of the most modern wind tunnels in Formula One. As Toet said, 'We will be able to simulate the vibration of the car as it bounces over the road. We'll also be able to run a 50 per cent or full-scale model. Williams was the first to be able to investigate changes involving cornering. Now we will have the facility to measure cornering and steering capability. We will also have more accurate results as we will be able to measure the air pressure at more specific points than other wind tunnels. This will help us to maximize the aerodynamic efficiency of the car.'

AUSTRIA
SCHUMACHER WAS HAVING A GREAT RACE, UNTIL ...

After the setbacks at Monza, Ferrari had great hope for the next two races, the Austrian Grand Prix and the Luxembourg Grand Prix (held at the German Nurburgring). For one of the senior personnel at Ferrari, the race in Austria meant returning to his home country. Gustav Brunner, then head of research and development, has always had the same objective – to make the car go quicker. 'We start at the tip of the nose, then work through solving problems and looking at new ways of doing things. Sometimes we work on the existing car and sometimes the new car. We are fortunate in that we do not have pressure to produce a car. We have more time to think so we can be creative. We are the only department that has the freedom to dream.'

What about the change in regulations for 1998? 'With less grip from the tyres, we are putting more effort into developing the suspension. I think this will favour Schumacher as with less grip there will be more drifting and more need for control. It will not depend on the car so much, now it will be more of a Drivers' Championship than an Engineers' Championship.'

On the Saturday, Michael Schumacher qualified in ninth position, just as he had at Monza two weeks earlier. However, this time round he was having a great race, lying third with a strong possibility of finishing second behind Villeneuve, when team-mate Eddie Irvine was involved in an accident with Jean Alesi. This caused the yellow flag to be waved but Schumacher, who was behind Frentzen, didn't see it and overtook the Williams driver. It is illegal to overtake another car when the yellow flag, which indicates a dangerous situation on the track, is waved. For Schumacher, the result of breaching this regulation was a 10-second penalty, which put him back to ninth place. But all was not lost and Schumacher fought back to sixth place, overtaking Damon Hill on the very last lap to gain one point.

Eddie Irvine's crash with Jean Alesi started a war of words after both drivers retired from the race. Alesi went storming off towards the Ferrari garage declaring, 'I'm going to hit him. I don't understand what goes through a driver's head when he does things like that. He's crazy.'

Irvine was just as dismissive. 'I was overtaking him on the outside when he touched a wheel and flew into the air. He's a fruitcake and unstable.'

The sad conclusion to Austria from Ferrari's point of view was that Schumacher's lead in the Drivers' Championship was reduced to just one point, while Williams took over at the head of the Constructors' table with a 12-point advantage. Nigel Stepney was thinking about the press. 'We didn't get destroyed after Monza which is unusual. I think the press have seen that we can win. Last year I didn't speak to many of them. They've learnt that if they give us hassle, we'll say less. However, a leopard never changes its spots.'

The team, however, had been much more together during 1997 than 1996. Stepney also feels that having all design functions in-house greatly improved relationships. 'Having dropped FDD and with everything moved to Maranello, I think the working environment is a lot better. If the people above you are calm and stable, then it makes everyone else more relaxed. The arrival of Ross Brawn was beneficial. Michael and Eddie also help by not using the press to complain about the team.

'Everyone has a lot more respect for their colleagues. Before with FDD, we lost so much time talking and not actually doing anything. John [Barnard] didn't want to trust anyone and give anybody experience. We're now taking on all aspects of the car and we're doing all the design at Maranello, and that's a big step for us. We make mistakes but we have enough experience and time to keep it all under control. Now we can find the answers and cure the problems.'

Back in the Formula One offices, Luana Piccinini and Anna

Maria Consani are keeping things moving as the phone and fax constantly ring, bringing information and demanding answers. Luana is Claudio Berro's personal assistant, while Anna Maria looks after Jean Todt. Luana says, 'The number of requests from foreign journalists has increased enormously. We always try to accommodate the requests and make sure that each country gets access to us.'

Mauro Boreggio is the personnel man who had taken over from Stefano Domenicali. 'The important thing is to keep positive, without going over the top in celebrating if we win or falling into a depression if we lose. We must keep to the general strategy.'

REACHING THE CENTURY
LUXEMBOURG WAS SCHUMACHER'S 100TH GP

Next on the Formula One calendar was the Luxembourg Grand Prix, held at the Nurburgring in Germany. It marked the 100th Grand Prix for Michael Schumacher. So how did that make him feel? 'Old! It always used to be my predecessors like Nigel Mansell who were celebrating 100 Grands Prix. Now it's me.'

Frank Williams, sitting next to Schumacher at a press conference, was in a devilish mood before the race. When asked about the possibilities of his man Villeneuve winning the Drivers' Championship, he admitted, 'The only problem on the horizon is sitting two metres to my left.' When asked about the one-point difference that separated his driver from Schumacher he was quick on the draw. 'We will strengthen our suspension.' A timely reminder of the Schumacher–Hill accident in Australia, during the last race of the 1994 season and a canny insight into the future.

At the Nurburgring, Schumacher qualified fifth and Irvine

14th. Ahead of the two Ferraris, Villeneuve was second with Frentzen third. Schumacher was not happy: 'It's worrying to have the two Williams in front of me. It will be an advantage if Frentzen is in front of me and Villeneuve. Hakkinen [in pole position] could help me by winning the race.'

One thing Michael Schumacher wasn't expecting was a boot up the backside from his little brother. But that was exactly what happened. As the race started and the cars went into the first corner, Schumacher Senior pulled alongside Giancarlo Fisichella but then found brother Ralf going faster around the outside of both of them. Michael wisely switched to the outside, which left Ralf to continue his charge into the corner with Fisichella. The two Jordans collided and Ralf flew across the track and landed on brother Michael's car, breaking a suspension arm on the Ferrari in the process. Michael staggered on for another two laps before retiring. He stormed into the team truck where he was joined 20 minutes later by Ralf. Both brothers admitted it was a racing accident, but Michael was obviously devastated. 'It is a shame that the incident happened with my brother, but I don't think anyone is to blame for what happened as it was not a deliberate move. These things can happen and that is motor racing.'

Eddie Irvine's car died on him after 22 laps, and that was that for Ferrari. The two McLarens were leading when one by one they both had engine failures. That left Villeneuve in the lead and on his way to 10 points. However, Jean Todt will not give up until the battle is well and truly over. He summed the race up by saying, 'We could not have had a worse result. The other cars in the race did not help our cause. However, while it is still mathematically possible for us to win the Championship, we will try as hard as we can right to the end.'

Niki Lauda gave his usual blunt opinion. 'Ralf is completely mad. When I saw him up beside his brother I said to myself, "What's he doing?" If he'd used his head he wouldn't have caused an accident like that. I've never seen anything like it.'

After Nurburgring it was time to re-group before the final two deciding races in Japan and Spain ... and a nerve-wracking climax to the season for Ferrari.

A BREATHTAKING FINALE
THERE WERE NO HYSTERICS, JUST SILENCE

In Japan, strategy was always going to be vital for Ferrari after the news that Jacques Villeneuve would be racing under appeal following an incident in the Saturday morning practice session, when he ignored a yellow flag. The spectre of being stripped of any points he would gain in the race was sure to influence his, and therefore Ferrari's, race tactics.

The hero of the weekend was Eddie Irvine. Finally shaking off his fear of qualifying, he came good at the right moment to take third place on the grid. 'I think testing has helped,' said Irvine. 'The team understands now what I need from the car. I cannot tolerate mid-corner understeer. As I turn in, I'm more progressive on the throttle. Also, I've just realized that I needed more front wing to make handling better.'

Schumacher qualified on the front row of the grid. For Villeneuve on pole position, having one Ferrari by his side and the other behind him was not a comforting experience, and so it proved.

At the start of the race, the Canadian made an aggressive move across the track and blocked Schumacher from overtaking him into the first corner. Once in the lead, it became clear that Villeneuve was on a go-slow strategy.

As one Ferrari manager said, 'Villeneuve was driving as

though he expected to lose any points gained from this race, so his idea was to hold us up. It was very silly, as when Eddie got past him, he had Michael right up behind him and no time advantage when coming into the pits. When the Williams team messed up his second pit stop and he lost five seconds, it just put him further into trouble.'

The Ferrari plan was to have Irvine behind Villeneuve, so that if the Canadian tried anything untoward, he could compensate leaving Schumacher's bid for the World Championship in tact. So on lap 2, at the start of the first turn, Schumacher backed off enough to slow down Hakkinen behind him, a manoeuvre that allowed Irvine to overtake both drivers, and then set upon the hapless Villeneuve.

By the end of the third lap, the Irishman had passed Villeneuve (Irvine: 'I told Michael before the race that it was possible to overtake there on the outside, but he thought it wasn't – too slippery, he said') and sped away into the distance, opening up a staggering lead of 12 seconds after three more laps.

After the first pit stop, Irvine remained well ahead, but with Schumacher now just in front of Villeneuve. It was then that Irvine 'received the calling' on his car radio and slowed down so that by lap 25, in exactly the same place as before, Schumacher took over in front again, a lead he was never to relinquish as Irvine closed the door on Villeneuve. For the Canadian it was downhill all the way, as a disastrous second pit stop saw him drop from third to seventh place.

The performance of Villeneuve and Frentzen in Japan suggested that the Williams drivers hardly knew each other. Frentzen finally woke up half-way through the race and started to challenge Schumacher, but it was too late, and despite Damon Hill's apparent blocking tactics (Brawn: 'It wasn't particularly fair, but he must have had his reasons'), Schumacher was first past the line to claim what he described as 'one of the most important victories of my career'.

So it was first and third for the Ferrari drivers, who were quick to congratulate each other after the race. 'I told you that you could go around the outside at turn six,' said a cheeky Irvine to Schumacher. Ross Brawn was delighted. 'For our pit stop strategy, we had to change things around on the second stop. Michael was going to come in first when he found himself behind traffic, but then he managed to get past and so we brought in Eddie first instead. We had to act fast!'

A dejected Villeneuve finished in fifth place and saw his lead in the Drivers' Championship cut to one point, pending his appeal. One small consolation for Williams was winning the Constructors' Championship. The Ferrari team was generous in its praise: 'We must be honest and say that the best constructor won.'

THE FINAL SHOWDOWN
VILLENEUVE WAS SHOWING THE STRAIN

And so to Jerez, in Spain, and the final showdown between Schumacher and Villeneuve. Williams decided to withdraw its appeal against Villeneuve's ban the week before, which meant that Schumacher had a one-point lead in the Championship going into the last race of the 1997 season. Suzuka hero Eddie Irvine was in no doubt about his role. 'I'm going to help Michael in Jerez. It's in my contract. If I don't, then I won't get paid. It's as simple as that!'

By the Saturday of the European Grand Prix weekend, Jacques Villeneuve was showing the strain. At the end of the morning's free practice, he rushed over to Irvine, who was

TELEMETRY

Ferrari works closely with sponsors Magneti Marelli on the telemetry, which feeds back technical data from the car to screens back at the garage. A receiver takes information from the car while a transmitter sends information to a point just outside the team garage. From the receiver on the garage wall, the information is passed along a cable to the modem box. This box transforms up to half a million bits of data into readable form. There are up to 128 different parameters. Each parameter relates to one piece of information – for example, the speed of the car, oil pressure, fuel consumption, battery voltage and air pressure.

sitting in his car, and accused the Irishman of blocking him for three or four corners. 'F***ing idiot!' he screamed, before storming into the neighbouring Williams garage. 'I don't know what he'll do next,' said Villeneuve later. 'He doesn't like other drivers. We all know he's a clown, but there's no need to play like that.'

Irvine was dismissive. 'No one can possibly think that Villeneuve deserves to win the Championship. Schumacher is the best driver.'

Qualifying was electric. Villeneuve on pole, Schumacher second and Frentzen third, all with exactly the same 1 minute 21.072 qualifying time – never before in the history of Formula One had that happened. Schumacher was pleased to be on the front row. 'The start will be crucial,' he said. And the German gave himself a brilliant chance by powering ahead of Villeneuve into the first corner, with Frentzen creating a surprise by also pulling in front of his Williams team-mate. By the end of the first lap, Schumacher already had a two-second lead, but on lap 7, Frentzen allowed Villeneuve through into second to put pressure on the Ferrari. Meanwhile, Eddie Irvine was in seventh place and making little impression on the leading pack.

It soon became clear that both Ferrari and Williams were on a two-stop strategy when Schumacher came in to the pits on lap 22, followed by Villeneuve a lap later. Frentzen was now in the lead and was doing his best to hold up Schumacher after the latter emerged from the pits ahead of Villeneuve. But Frentzen was soon forced to go into the pits for re-fuelling, which left the two protagonists for the World Championship alone out at the front in a head-to-head fight.

By lap 44, both drivers had made their second pit stops with Villeneuve starting to make ground on Schumacher. Four laps later, the battle was over. Villeneuve attempted to take Schumacher on the inside of Dry Sac; the German kept to his racing line, but then as Villeneuve edged ahead he tried to shut the door. Too late. Schumacher's front right wheel hit the side pod of the Williams, and the Ferrari ended up on the gravel and unable to restart. At first, the worry from the Williams garage was that its Championship had also been wrecked, but Villeneuve managed to nurse his car round the remaining 21 laps to finish the race third behind the McLarens of Hakkinen and Coulthard – and more importantly gain a precious four Championship-winning points.

For Ferrari, the hopes and dreams of a Formula One Drivers' World Championship lay in ruins. The mechanics were devastated and an eerie silence descended over the garage. Two-and-a-half hours after the race had ended, Schumacher finally spoke. "I've had happier days in my life, but that's racing. I was always ahead of him [Villeneuve] and able to keep him behind me. He made an opportune move, which went well for him and badly for me. I braked on the maximum limit and he braked later. If he had stayed behind me he would have lost the Championship, so he had to make a move. To be honest, I would have done the same.'

Jean Todt was bitterly disappointed, but not beaten. 'We didn't expect to be in contention for the Championship but with Michael Schumacher driving for us we were up at the top. I believe he will drive for Ferrari for many years.'

There were no hysterics outside the Ferrari garage, just silence. As Ross Brawn pointed out, 'Ferrari must remember how far they've come, not that they've lost a Championship they were never expected to win at the beginning of the season.'

Shirts were exchanged between the teams as the Williams party got underway. A few members of the Ferrari team looked on longingly. One day...

However, the Scuderia were on their way back: five Grand Prix wins this year with Schumacher, on 78 points, just three behind the newly crowned champion Jacques Villeneuve. And in 1998, the car would be made entirely in Maranello.

● ● ●

The V10 engine roared for the last time as Eddie Irvine's car was examined. The Irishman had finished fifth, but the real prize was still to come. Nigel Stepney paused for thought, then took a deep breath. 'We'll be back next year. Then watch out.' The legend lives on.

CHAPTER TEN

In the Deep Midwinter

'The car is completely different. I can see a lot of Rory Byrne's signature, while it still keeps the good ideas of John Barnard.'

Michael Schumacher
on the new 1998 Ferrari

Formula One has a split personality. During the racing season it's all about sun, jet set travel and beautiful people. In the winter the beautiful people disappear and the real people get down to work. This means testing – and it isn't glamorous.

On 15 January 1998, Michael Schumacher was due to test at Fiorano, the Ferrari test track. It was a cold, wet, miserable day and to make matters worse, the surrounding area was greeted with nothing but silence. Bad news. When the Ferrari is testing it can be heard all around the town – from the green grocer's to the school. When there is silence Schumacher usually does a runner back to Switzerland, Monaco or wherever he fancies. Schumacher had been scheduled to give only a couple of select interviews, but the day passed in a series of phone calls. We were told, 'He's gone shopping', 'He'll be here about four o'clock', 'He'll be here in ten minutes', 'He'll be here in five minutes', then silence. Finally, a bright yellow Fiat coupé leapt out of the tunnel at ferocious speed, did a twirl round the corner and came to a swift halt in front of Enzo Ferrari's house. Schumi had arrived.

A slim, angular man, he put on his Dekra hat, did a German TV interview, then turned to me. 'Could we talk in the gym?' By this stage, having stood in the freezing cold for what seemed like hours, I didn't care if we talked in the local bar, so long as we talked.

Five minutes later Superman Schumacher reappeared in the gym decked in his 'workout gear'. Stepping on to the Technogym running machine, it was obvious he still had a lot of aggression to dispel, and most of it was centred on the infamous Villeneuve incident that had occurred during the pair's down-to-the-wire fight during the last race of the 1997 season. Although it is now water under the bridge,

Schumacher was clearly still chewing over what might have been: 'He braked late into the corner and he would have gone wide, and if I'd got through I would have taken him on the inside.'

But he didn't and Williams will run with 1 and 2 on its cars in 1998, and Ferrari with 3 and 4. *C'est la vie*. Life moves on and there's always another year. 'If all goes as we think, I should be on target to win the World Championship this year. We now have the right people in the right place. This year is the first year we have the new guy's [Rory Byrne's] car and the World Championship has to be our target.'

The previous designer John Barnard had, of course, thrown in the towel and left the stable of the prancing horse at the beginning of 1997. The 1998 car was the first from Rory Byrne, and he and Schumacher had already worked together at Benetton. The German was optimistic: 'The car is completely different. I can see a lot of Rory Byrne's signature while keeping the good ideas of John Barnard. John Barnard is much better at design — aerodynamics is probably his weakest side.'

THE HUMAN TOUCH
OUT OF THE CAR, THEY'RE DIFFERENT

A brilliant driver, Schumacher is often accused of clouding that brilliance with arrogant behaviour, but it is the unpredictability of his fellow drivers that sometimes leaves him cold. He has been hurt by Jacques Villeneuve's constant jibes. 'Apparently, Jacques has changed compared to when we last spoke immediately after the race at Jerez. He's got my home telephone number, so I don't know why he didn't call me. We had a great night after Jerez. In fact I've had a couple

A PROBLEM OF STRESS

Easing the physical burdens of stress at Ferrari are the two team doctors, Fredrick Fernando and Alessandro Biffi. Both of them work at the Sports Science Institute of the Italian National Olympic Committee based in Rome. Fred and Alessandro follow the team at the Grands Prix to ensure that if necessary there is a physician ready and available. They also run a yearly screening programme for all team members in Maranello. Once a month the team physicians are present in Maranello, and if necessary other specialists are called in.

The mechanics have to withstand a lot of stress, including travelling, irregular and often long hours and the pressure of performing at a consistently high level in very short periods of time (such as pit stops). Despite this Fred was surprised at what he discovered. 'The mechanics at Maranello are in extremely good shape. Some can actually be compared to top-level endurance athletes.' They also have the advantage of enjoying a Mediterranean diet.

of great nights with him after races. That's why I like him. You have a great fight and then you have a drink together. If this is going to change, I don't care. There are other people you can have a drink with.'

If the world of motor racing is two-faced, Schumacher finds solace in his home life. Wife Corinna and baby daughter, Gina Maria are his reference points, and his family is due to expand with the news that the pair are currently expecting another baby. During the winter, Schumacher has concentrated on his fitness and spent time with his adored daughter. 'She has developed amazingly during the last two months. She's crawling and has started walking by trying to pull herself up. She doesn't want to be fed anymore, insisting on doing it herself.'

A little of the Schumacher determination perhaps? 'Yes, she is more like me in character. I was very active as a baby and Gina Maria loves to move around, walk around and be busy. Corinna was a quiet baby. Being married and having a child makes you different. When things go wrong it makes it better that things are going right at home.'

Things are also going right at work in that Schumacher finally has a team-mate he gets on with: 'A lot of drivers get mentally broken against me but Eddie has overcome that. From my career point of view, Eddie is my best team-mate. He's not like Johnny [Herbert, who drove with him at Benetton during the 1995 season]. He would be complaining all year and talking to Ross [Brawn]. Johnny might not like to hear that, but that's how it is.'

Eddie Irvine has also brought a sense of humour to Ferrari and an ability to take the sting out of tense situations. He and Schumacher enjoy a mutual respect, even though they are unlikely to meet much away from the track. Schumacher laughs as he says: 'Eddie's a great guy, but we have different lifestyles. He's not very interested in family life and I'm not interested in being a playboy.'

SERIOUS TALK
THIS IS THE WATERSHED YEAR

The chat changed to the 1998 season. This is the watershed year. The year when it should all come together and Ferrari should once again be at the pinnacle of success.

Schumacher, with his precise prediction powers, thought

that Ferrari's main rival would be McLaren. 'Mika Hakkinen was unlucky a few times last year so perhaps his luck will change.' Perhaps indeed! But it wasn't too difficult to predict that McLaren would be leading contenders for the 1998 Championship. Adrian Newey, acknowledged as the most brilliant aerodynamicist in the sport, had moved from Williams to McLaren. The aerodynamics, tyres and engine are vital to the success of the car so if you've got the best guy on board in one of these areas you've definitely got a head start – added to which McLaren had chosen to go with Bridgestone tyres rather than Goodyear, and Bridgestone were making noises about having the best tyre package.

● ● ●

So that just left the engine ... and at the first race it wasn't looking too good.

CHAPTER ELEVEN

The 1998 Season Begins

'The first race is important as it gives a good base to build on ... Eddie showed that there was potential.'

Nigel Stepney
after the 1998 Australian Grand Prix

At Melbourne, host to the first Grand Prix of the 1998 season, it soon became apparent that the McLarens of Mika Hakkinen and David Coulthard were not just quicker than the rest of the cars, they were *miles* quicker. To confirm the point, Hakkinen qualified in pole position with Coulthard second. Schumacher was some 7/10ths of a second off the pace and consequently found himself on the third row of the grid.

By the fifth lap of the race – at which point he was in third position, despite being a massive 14 seconds behind Hakkinen – Schumacher's engine blew, leaving him furious and frustrated.

Meanwhile, Eddie Irvine, who had used the spare car for the race, was eighth at the start – a position he held until the first pit stop. But pit stops are a crucial part of racing strategy, and by the time all the drivers had finished pitting Irvine had moved up to fourth place, where he stayed until the chequered flag.

A pre-race agreement between the two McLaren drivers allowing whichever driver was leading into the first corner to stay ahead of the other, meant that, despite Coulthard leading the Australian Grand Prix for some time, he magnanimously slowed down to let his team-mate by and take the first victory of the season. After such a decisive first and second place by the McLaren team, and as is typical of Formula One, accusations and gossip were already flying around the paddock. Were McLaren's brakes legal? Could one driver let his team-mate through in such an obvious way? Would Ferrari fight back in Brazil?

On top of all that, the Goodyear tyres came in for some heavy criticism, but things were not as bad as they appeared. Goodyear had put in an enormous effort during the winter and Perry Bell, the Formula One operations manager, was ready to defend the situation. 'We struggled in winter testing, but we made a breakthrough in the compound for the rear tyre, and then we had to concentrate on the front tyres. We have found them to be too narrow, so we are making them wider. We will both [Ferrari and Goodyear] work on improving the whole package of tyres and car.'

Bell was backed up by Irvine who declared, 'I am happy with the tyres. Goodyear have worked well. We made one stop [in Australia] and all the cars on Bridgestone made two.'

Yet it might have been possible for Irvine to have finished third and taken a place on the podium had his pit stop not presented problems. As Jean Todt explained, 'Eddie had a good race. But at the pit stop, he did not manage to get away cleanly as he could not select first gear because the engine revs were too high. This probably cost him the chance of a podium finish.'

Todt was also disappointed to see the huge gap between the McLarens and the rest of the field. But his attitude was to knuckle down and get on with it. 'This is the first race [of the season] and there is a big gap between the winning team and the rest. There is no point in talking about it; we must remain calm and get on with our job.'

However, Chief Mechanic Nigel Stepney could not hide his disappointment: 'It was a bad way to start. The first race is important as it gives a good base to build on. Having an engine failure was a low point and not a good start, but Eddie showed that there was potential. He finished fourth.'

Schumacher watched the race from the pit wall, where he could only gaze in wonder at the pace of the McLarens. However, the battle was new and there was a long way to go. 'We mustn't exaggerate the situation. McLaren were on a two-stop strategy and we were on one, so it was normal they were much faster. Now we just have to go back to work, sort out the problems and get it right.'

Schumacher was putting on a brave face, but behind the scenes the situation was a little different. His race engineer, Ignazio Lunetta, admits that the German was still suffering the effects of the terrible end to the 1997 season. 'Michael was depressed in the motorhome after Melbourne. He thought we'd start off winning and he'd be able to put aside any thoughts of 1997, but it wasn't to be. He still thought about it and felt bad, and only a win would help him recover from the guilt. We all thought we'd be in a good position, but we found we were behind McLaren with a lot of work to do, so it wasn't a good start.'

LATIN TOUCHDOWN
MAKING AN IMPACT IN BRAZIL AND ARGENTINA

And so to São Paolo in Brazil for the second race of the season. The bumpy circuit has never been easy on the Ferraris, and the Saturday qualifying session served as a reminder – if one were needed – that the McLaren cars were currently in a class of their own.

Once again, Hakkinen qualified in pole position, with Schumacher fourth on the grid, more than a full second behind the Finn. Irvine was close to his team-mate in sixth, but with only one updated engine available (the 047/D), which went to Schumacher, and having to contend with a nasty attack of 'flu, the experience of the race for the Irishman was less than joyful.

As a result of the Australian Grand Prix, the FIA banned obvious overtaking manoeuvres between team-mates, yet this decision had caused some confusion. After all, Formula One is a team sport, and there were dark mutterings about having to tear up contracts and missing the point in having a Number One and Number Two driver. However, as we will see later in the season, it was pretty much left up to the teams to cover up overtaking manoeuvres between team-mates. If they could get away with it, then all right; if it was too obvious, they'd risk being called before the FIA Committee.

Despite feeling unwell, Irvine made a fantastic start shooting into fourth place ahead of Schumacher, who dropped to fifth. However, the German soon took fourth place away from Irvine, then, from the start of lap 10, began to close on Frentzen. Things went fairly smoothly until Schumacher's second pit stop on lap 53, during which his engine stalled. However, the mechanics reacted quickly and he was soon out on the track again, rejoining ahead of Frentzen in third place. The two McLarens were, unsurprisingly, running first and second.

After the Australian race, team boss Jean Todt said that changes would be made, and they were. Schumacher was running with a new, comparatively untried engine; it had been a risk, but it paid off. Slowly, it was all beginning to come together, and the engine was a big step forward. Paolo Martinelli, head of the Engine department, agreed it had been a positive step. 'Maybe we took a bit of a risk running a new engine in the race, but it had gone well in practice and qualifying, and we needed to take that risk. Now we have to work hard to improve the performance while maintaining reliability.'

However, the tyre performance still needed some improvement. Goodyear planned to have its new wider front tyres ready for the next race at Argentina and there was talk that these tyres would give an improvement of 7/10ths of a second a lap. Jean Todt was well aware of the situation: 'We have to do better. We are second [behind McLaren] but we want to be first. That was our objective at the start of 1998. The continuous development of the car never stops, we have to look forward.'

Relieved with his third position, Schumacher was slightly exuberant on the podium, with the result that he slipped on some champagne and had to be helped to his feet by Hakkinen. However, Hakkinen's gentlemanly behaviour off the track did not mean he'd be giving way on it. The season was going to be long and hard.

One big change from the point of view of personnel was that Giorgio Ascanelli had decided to alter his job description and remain at the factory rather than travel with the team. 'I am grateful to the company for giving me the opportunity to spend more time with my family,' he said. But it was also in the company's interests to keep Ascanelli back in the factory. Ferrari needed a strong and experienced person to direct operations when the team was at the track.

Soon a brand new high-tech motorhome would be making its debut and this would further facilitate contact between track and factory. Ascanelli is pragmatic and aware of the importance of the Schumacher factor. 'We have the best driver and I think that 80 per cent of our progress is due to the driver. It is also a tremendous advantage to have everything under one roof (design, and research and development) as we can achieve more. There is no dead time due to discussions between us and Ferrari UK in Shalford. Now we've had a year of all working together here, we can see the benefits.'

As for Schumacher, finally he could begin to put the disasters of 1997 behind him. 'I am convinced that Ferrari will be competitive very quickly and so our objective is still the World Championship. The road is long and those two in front

[Hakkinen and Coulthard] could fall off the pace sooner or later. It's clear that the recovery depends above all on us and I have great faith in our ability.'

An Easter Sunday of miracles saw both Ferraris on the podium — Schumacher first and Irvine third — after the Argentinian Grand Prix. And the team couldn't have chosen a better place for victory with the high number of Italian immigrants helping to celebrate as though the race had been on their own home ground. In just two races, Ferrari had risen from no hopers to Championship contenders.

On lap 2 Schumacher was in second place and Irvine fourth, the German taking the lead on lap 5 with Hakkinen and Irvine behind him. Positions did not change until lap 28 when Michael made his first pit stop, with Eddie stopping one lap later. They rejoined in second and fifth places respectively, Irvine moving up to fourth when Coulthard pitted and third after Villeneuve re-fuelled on lap 37. Hakkinen made his only stop on lap 42, handing Schumacher the lead, which he maintained even when he made his second stop on lap 53, staying ahead of Hakkinen by two seconds. Ten laps from the end it began to rain lightly and on lap 67 Michael went straight across the grass but kept his lead.

A non-fatal incident between Schumacher and Coulthard when the two cars touched briefly ensured that the race would be contentious, with accusations of Jerez 97 being thrown at the German. However, most informed observers felt it was a racing incident and should be regarded as that. The new tyres showed notable progress and the team had renewed confidence in its ability to challenge for the 1998 World Championship.

Ferrari's two-stop strategy as opposed to McLaren's one stop was an important contribution to victory and a sign of

Ross Brawn's tactical brilliance. After a year, Brawn was settled at Ferrari, imposing his calm, methodical approach on the team. 'I have to say that Ferrari is more sensible than it is perceived on the outside. It's no different to any other team; there is the same pressure to improve the car, and to do that you need to react quickly and work hard. Things have turned out better than I thought. Jean Todt had put a lot in place before I arrived and we are fairly close to what we want.'

Brawn was also relieved to have everything under one roof. 'We now have a reference point on the technical side. There is a great difference in having things separated between the UK and Italy and having it all here. Rory [Byrne] and I have clear lines of communication and reference. We have created a methodical approach, which is critical in any Formula One team. You have to make sure that an improvement is actually an improvement and modifications to the car are not made too soon because of the pressure to find something new.'

Both Ross Brawn and Rory Byrne know Michael Schumacher well, having worked with him at Benetton and, like Giorgio Ascanelli, they are both aware of just how much a driver of Schumacher's calibre can contribute to the team. Says Brawn, 'Michael adds 3 or 4/10ths of a second a lap to the car, and he works hard with the team. He isn't a driver who just appears for the race then disappears immediately after it. He stays and works it out with the rest of us. We got so close to the championship last year that I think people's belief in themselves is good now. We know we can do it.'

Rory Byrne looks at Schumacher from a designer's point of view, and, unlike John Barnard who didn't have an altogether easy relationship with Schumacher, he is completely in tune with his Number One driver. 'His 100 per cent speed is legendary, but he has other qualities that make the difference between a good driver and a World Champion. He has the ability to focus on areas of the car that need to be improved. If we develop a new system he can give precise feedback. He is also very good at adapting his driving style to get the best out of the car. He just seems to have the instinctive knowledge of doing what is right for the car. Very few drivers can do that.'

ON HOME GROUND
THE FANS HAD TASTED VICTORY

Next stop, the San Marino Grand Prix, held in Imola – and the pressure would be on in the race that is closest to the Ferrari home at Maranello. As the team returned from Argentina there was the feeling that maybe the tide was turning and the McLarens were, in fact, beatable. Nigel Stepney was happy with the ways things were going. 'The team has self-confidence, as we know we can win. There is no need for anyone to stick the knife in as we are all working together. With self-confidence you can go forward, and as long as we don't get over confident, we will continue to progress.'

Schumacher was the one to put it all into perspective. 'To win doesn't mean you are the best. I have been for one day; now we'll have to see. Obviously, I hope to be the best on other days. I think it will be a great struggle, and a great Championship.' And so it was to be.

Back at Imola, the fans had been given the taste of a win – and they wanted more. It was time to keep calm and move forward, even though it seemed as if the McLarens would steal the show. Coulthard was on pole position with Hakkinen second; both Ferraris were behind them on the second row.

AN IDEAL PARTNERSHIP

The lubricant for the Ferrari engine supplied by Shell also plays a vital part in the design and development of Formula One racing cars. According to Ferrari Chief Designer, Rory Byrne: 'We have made a very significant improvement on the gearbox, which is due to the development of a lubricant that runs cooler than before. If we are dissipating less heat in the gearbox, the oil cooler can be smaller. This helps with weight saving, and also with aerodynamic efficiency.'

Byrne is also excited about the potential of the new hydraulic oils being developed by Shell. 'There are new oils under development, which will help the performance of all the hydraulic components, from the brake balance system and the engine throttle and trumpets through to the gear shift and the power steering.'

The close relationship between Ferrari and Shell is highlighted by the one-to-one contact between Ferrari engineers and Shell personnel, in terms or research and development, logistics and at the track.

Shell has also created some stunning advertising with Ferrari, including an ambitious project shot in the Mojave Desert. The scenario is this: a huge transporter plane flies in low over the Ferrari Formula One car, which is driven by Nicola Larini. With both aircraft and car hurtling along at high speed, a re-fuelling line emerges from the plane to link up with the car. After filling is complete, the plane flies off into the distance. This awe-inspiring image was not a computer simulation and filming took place on a normal road.

The 120,000 fans who had turned up to watch their Ferrari heroes weren't disappointed. Schumacher was third at the start with Eddie fifth. Eddie was later able to capitalize on his first pit stop, coming out on the track ahead of Villeneuve into third place. After the shakedown of the second round of pit stops, and with Hakkinen having to retire with a gearbox problem, Coulthard and Schumacher were left to fight it out for victory. In a period of 15 laps, Schumacher managed to reduce the gap between him and Coulthard by 15 seconds. It looked as though he could do it, and snatch a second victory, but he just ran out of time and had to be satisfied with second – the same as last year, when the Ferraris had finished second and third.

Jean Todt, although cautious, saw this as another step towards the Championship. After the race he declared, 'Hakkinen's failure to finish the race isn't by chance. Under pressure the McLarens can break. But we have to grow. It was great to see two Ferrari drivers on the podium in front of our fans, but we aren't completely satisfied. We have to understand why the last set of tyres performed the best.'

But things were getting better. 'After four races we are getting better from a technical point of view. We have made a step forward even if we are not yet near the McLarens.' Once again the strategy was decisive. Irvine was fighting Villeneuve for fourth place and, as Todt explained, 'We decided to put less fuel in Irvine's car. The pit stop was quicker and Eddie got away and finished third.'

There were new modifications on the car including the famous 'candelabra', the side wings. Says Todt, 'They give us a more balanced aerodynamic load. From Tuesday [following the race] we'll be testing quite a few things at Barcelona including this.'

It was difficult to see if Imola could be classified as a triumph or not. There was no doubt that progress was being made, but the McLarens were still very strong. As Schumacher admitted, 'The real luck at Imola was that Hakkinen, the man who counts the most, did not finish. Now we are all closer, the Championship is open.'

Also open for discussion was Schumacher's contract with Ferrari. The stable of the prancing horse wanted to keep both Jean Todt and Michael for the rest of their careers. The German admitted, 'We have not talked a lot about this, but the contract is always under discussion. I am happy to know that the team is pleased with my work to the point of thinking about extending our collaboration. Let's wait and see.'

●   ●   ●

Wili Weber, Schumacher's manager, would shortly be in serious discussion with the double World Champion about his driver's contract, but for now all effort would be focussed on winning the World Championship, and the next race was in Spain.

CHAPTER TWELVE

A Winning Combination

'There needs to be a balance between money and the joy of racing.'

Giorgio Ascanelli

At Barcelona in Spain, McLaren continued its domination of the 1998 Formula One season. Hakkinen qualified on pole position and Coulthard sat next to him in second. Meanwhile, Schumacher qualified third, with Eddie Irvine three places and just 6/10ths of a second behind him.

The race was another demonstration of McLaren supremacy. Things had looked promising for the two Ferraris, especially after Eddie's great start which moved him to third place, with Schumacher, though fifth, likely to progress further up the field. On lap 25 Irvine and Benetton's Giancarlo Fisichella both made pit stops. Schumacher pitted two laps later, joining the race in third place ahead of Irvine and Fisichella who collided on the following lap, both cars stopping in the gravel. Fisichella was convinced it was Irvine's fault and was ready for a heated debate. Irvine, demonstrating a more mature approach than he might previously have been recognized for, ignored the furious Italian and walked away from him back to the pits.

In the event, the stewards decided that Fisichella had acted inappropriately and he was fined $7,500, which did not improve his humour. 'What do you want me to say?' he said as he drove away from the circuit on his scooter. 'According to them [the stewards] I took Irvine off and so it was all my fault. I never thought of physically attacking Irvine ... but I was furious. Twice, at the start and after Schumacher's pit stop, Eddie came alongside me at the same place in the same corner and I let him pass. The first time I lifted my foot off the accelerator, but it wouldn't have taken much to have had him off the track. Then when I tried to pass him on the inside he came into me, ruining my car and his.'

Irvine, not noted for his diplomacy in such cases, showed a remarkable capacity for pouring oil on troubled water. 'It's normal that the authorities should intervene in such a case, but they've been too severe in the punishment,' he said. 'It's a real pity that Giancarlo must pay $7,500 for an accident that, although it could have been avoided, is still a racing accident.'

Irvine was upset to see his tremendous start vanish into thin air and Schumacher, despite his third place, was unhappy about the continuing McLaren domination. 'I think they probably worked better than us during the winter. It's true to say that they have a tyre advantage, but a big part of the performance is down to the car.'

Schumacher was also being plagued by a series of not very good starts, in addition to which he received a 10-second penalty for breaking the pit lane speed limit. 'I lost a couple of positions with wheelspin. I regained them after the first pit stop, but then had a problem with the pit lane speed limit. It was probably a malfunction of my limiter, but I don't know why it happened. The team performed a couple of great pit stops and after the second one, I re-entered the track ahead of Wurz.'

It was becoming more and more obvious that to be a front runner in Formula One you needed big money. Ferrari, McLaren, Williams and Benetton all have big budgets. Some of the smaller teams like Minardi would always find it hard to win, let alone have a World Champion, even if they had another Schumacher.

Back in the factory Giorgio Ascanelli was contemplating the importance of money. 'When I first started in motor racing, it wasn't so important. You could spend £5,000 on an engine, bolt it on the back of the car and win races. Now it is different. I suppose if there is no entertainment the money will go down, and everyone will have similar money. Then the business comes in and the money goes up. There needs to be a balance between money and the joy of racing. We have to come to terms with the law and tobacco, and then we have to move on to the next era.'

At least reliability had greatly improved and Ross Brawn, Ferrari technical director, paid tribute to supplier Shell. 'Without a serious partner like Shell we wouldn't be as good in terms of performance and reliability. There are two main areas: the performance side in which Shell provides an outstanding service with new fuels and lubricants, and then there is problem solving. We can now analyse all fluids at the circuit and pinpoint a problem before it becomes serious. That kind of support is critical to success in a sport in which winners and losers are defined by 100ths of a second.'

AND SO TO MONACO
TODT WAS IN BULLISH MOOD

Jean Todt was aware of the pressure to beat the all-conquering McLarens: 'I can't say I'm happy with third place; it's not the result we wanted, but we know that at the moment we can't do any more. We are working at 100 per cent. We have to look at an overall improvement in everything – chassis, brakes, engine, aerodynamics and obviously, tyres. The team worked very well in the pit stops allowing us to get to third [at Barcelona]. I am convinced that at Monte Carlo Schumacher will obtain a good result.'

Ross Brawn was bullish about Ferrari's chances at the famous street circuit of Monaco. He knew there were important modifications in the pipeline, particularly regarding the suspension. 'We need to be able to compete with the McLarens as soon as possible. If we delay it any longer the Championship will be over.'

However, Monaco is not an altogether happy place for Ferrari despite last year's race in the rain, which Schumacher dominated and won. The year before that he'd made a rare mistake and crashed the car before the race had barely got going. This year echoed that disappointment for Schumacher, but for Irvine things were better.

The result didn't help the Championship situation. Hakkinen won the race (his fourth victory in the first six races of the season), and went to the Palace to dance with the Monaco princesses enjoying a 26 point advantage in the Drivers' Championship. It looked like the 1998 winner was already decided.

Schumacher, fighting for a Championship he could see slipping away from his grasp, went for the jugular, but only succeeded in making a series of mistakes, finally limping home in 10th position. Starting from fourth on the grid, the German was third by lap 18, with Irvine fifth. Schumacher then pitted on lap 30, briefly losing third place for one lap, until Fisichella pitted on the next lap. On lap 37, Michael found Wurz in front of him and after a duel in which neither car would concede, they had a coming together that resulted in Michael having to return to the pits for a four-minute stop to repair his damaged rear suspension.

The German lost three laps and returned in 16th place. At the end of the race he ran straight into Pedro Diniz. Meanwhile, Irvine pitted on lap 45 and maintained his third place behind Fisichella to the flag.

Things were getting tense. No one could quite understand why Schumacher had risked hitting Wurz when he had a third place to protect. The excuses were becoming thinner on the ground, and the accusations about Schumacher's behaviour stronger. Some thought that his attack on Wurz was inadvisable, but his mistake with Diniz was inexcusable.

The young Brazilian was more surprised than angry at the tactics of the two-times World Champion. 'I don't understand his attack,' he said. 'He was a long way from me and by the time I saw him coming alongside me in the mirrors, it was too late. If I'd realised I would have let him pass – after all he was a lap behind me. At least I managed to limp past the chequered flag. If he'd pushed me out I would have been really angry.'

Wurz was a little more resigned: 'The coming together with Schumacher was just a normal race incident. There's no blame; we both tried to gain the best position.'

Schumacher was apparently being contradictory. After his win in Argentina he said, 'This Ferrari is very strong, it'll never break.' After Monaco he declared, 'It's necessary to build a stronger car!' – a rare criticism of his team, which showed the stress he was feeling at apparently always being second best.

Things weren't much easier on Irvine. Even though he finished third, he managed to take Frentzen out of the race at the Loews hairpin, much to the displeasure of the Williams driver. The fact that this was the first time Irvine had finished ahead of Schumacher (retirements excluded) since the two had become team-mates at Ferrari was somewhat lost in the general controversy.

Irvine was keeping a low profile on the incident with Frentzen. 'He was wide at Loews and I got inside him, and there was a small coming together,' said the Irishman. 'It wasn't very clear and I'll have to see it again on the video. When two cars enter a curve together this can happen.'

In the words of the song, 'Things can only get better' – and they were about to get a lot better. Eddie Irvine was having his best season with Ferrari — three podium positions so far — and his race engineer, Luca Baldisserri, had his own thoughts on this improved performance. 'The 1998 car is much more drivable. Rory [Byrne, the designer] has made the car much more stable. In 1996 and 1997 the drivers had been forced to drive in a certain way. The other thing is that this is our third year together as a group. We know each other well. At the end of last season Eddie took all his mechanics to Dublin for a weekend. We had a great time competing in kart races and playing football. Team building is very important and we all feel much more together as a result.'

But Eddie Irvine's personal success was still taking second place to the battle for the World Championship and in that department, things were looking no better.

After Monaco the team got down to some serious work testing at Monza and at Silverstone. Goodyear had taken its second-generation rear tyres to Monaco, but still seemed to be losing out to its competitor, Bridgestone, in the tyre war. In Argentina the Bridgestone option tyre had not been good so the gap had artificially closed. Now in the European races there was a lot of catching up to do, and Goodyear was working to get the edge. But Goodyear operations manager Perry Bell saw this as a challenge: 'If there's only one company in Formula One, there's always a more conservative approach. With two keen competitors there is a greater push to make changes and progress.'

There was also the fact that Goodyear had announced it would be pulling out of Formula One at the end of 1998, and this, too, was causing tension. The Goodyear Chairman, Sam Gibara, had made a statement to say that Goodyear would be leaving, and inspite of constant contact with Ferrari

Chairman, Luca di Montezemolo, and Williams boss, Frank Williams, there didn't seem much hope of changing his mind – much to the disappointment of everyone working in Formula One. The new grooved tyres had taken a bit of getting used to as Perry Bell explained: 'We were on a steep learning curve at the beginning of the year. At Magny-Cours [the French Grand Prix], we hope to be running the fourth-generation rear tyres.'

The Schumacher factor is a strong force, and Goodyear was being accused of showing favouritism towards Ferrari and the double World Champion. The new wider fronts had not made a huge difference to Williams but Goodyear still insisted it had been the right decision. After all, as Rory Byrne has said, Schumacher has a great ability to develop different areas of the car, and this was never more obvious than in tyre development. Perry Bell also confirmed Goodyear's willingness to listen to Schumacher's opinion. 'We like Schumacher to evaluate the changes and he does a confirmation run to establish if he's happy. If Schumacher didn't like the tyres we have to look at the situation very carefully. He has power, but the changes work on all the teams.'

FLYAWAY TO CANADA
AT LAST, THE SCENT OF VICTORY

Montreal, and at last the sweet scent of victory – although after qualifying it still looked as if the McLaren domination could not be broken. In the familiar story of the season to date, both cars qualified on the front row of the grid – Coulthard on pole, with Hakkinen second. Schumacher was right behind them in third, but Irvine languished in a lowly eighth.

The Canadian Grand Prix was a contentious race with two

starts – and despite winning the race, Schumacher was once again at the centre of controversy. At the first start, he made a clean getaway into second place, while Irvine made up one place into seventh. But the race was red flagged after an accident at the first corner involving Alexander Wurz, Jean Alesi and Jarno Trulli. Wurz, particularly, was extremely lucky to escape unhurt.

Another accident at the second start brought out the Safety Car. Hakkinen was forced to retire after only a few metres with a broken gearbox and on lap 5 when the Safety Car withdrew, Schumacher was in second place. The Safety Car was to make another appearance on lap 13 and again on lap 20, when Michael made a pit stop, rejoining in third place.

It was while rejoining the race after this pit stop that Schumacher unceremoniously knocked a furious Frentzen out of the race, by forcing him into the sand as he negotiated the corner. The stewards saw fit to punish the Ferrari driver by giving him a 10-second penalty. The level of punishment infuriated the Williams team who thought a much tougher penalty was called for. In fact, some thought that Schumacher should have been black flagged, which would have ended his race then and there – but he wasn't, and on lap 38 he once again reclaimed second place.

When Fisichella pitted on lap 44, Schumacher took the lead, which was where he stayed until he crossed the finishing line. Eddie, meanwhile, made his final stop on lap 55, when third, and maintained that position to the end. Goodyear tyres were a major contribution to the improvement.

After the press conference, Schumacher went to see Frentzen, and apologized. But for some that simply wasn't good enough. After the meeting, Schumacher said:

'Everything's all right. It wasn't my fault. I've explained everything. I didn't see Heinz-Harald, I only saw him when I was close to him. The stewards understood this and only gave me a 10-second penalty. I've apologized to Frentzen and I'm sorry for him. But my victory has no shadow; I worked hard to get it and so did the team, which was fantastic on the pit stops. We had competitive tyres from Goodyear and we have to continue along this road to achieve more improvement and work towards reaching McLaren's level.'

It was the 10th victory for Michael Schumacher with Ferrari, but resentment against him was building up and would explode over the coming weeks and months.

By the time Ferrari reached Magny-Cours, home to the French Grand Prix which was next on the calendar, it was on a roll. In France there were new front wings, a new aero package and a high cooling package. Nigel Stepney was kept busy co-ordinating the changes. The new front wings now enabled the balance to be changed during the pit stops, so if the car felt unbalanced it could be rectified in six seconds! The continuous development programme was in full swing. And to help progress the new satellite truck, made its entrance at the race. The truck would facilitate a constant link between the factory and the track. A satellite link-up meant that meetings could be held in the truck, and using the data from the telemetry and data from the tests, changes could be decided and problems solved.

It was yet another improvement in communications and proved the worth of having an engineer of the calibre of Giorgio Ascanelli back in the factory to direct operations. As Nigel Stepney says, 'The factory is now much more efficient with Giorgio in charge. The whole operation is much smoother.'

The addition of a video camera will mean that individual parts of the car can be seen and discussions held with the factory to achieve an almost instant solution. Stepney describes it as such: 'The truck is now the main brain of our operation. We have ideas and meetings, and everything spreads out from there. That's why the truck is air-conditioned. There's so much thinking going on that the heat builds up and we need to keep it cool!'

Things were coming together but it was mid-season. As Stepney says, 'If we could start ahead of the field at the beginning of the season things would be better, but we are getting quicker each year.'

Unfortunately, Schumacher went off the track during the first practice session on Friday, so a long night was spent completing repairs on the chassis, including a new front wing, undertray and side pods. The mechanics, led by Nigel Stepney, were at the circuit by 6 am on Saturday to finish the front wing end plates.

Schumacher lost most of the second session of free practice on the Saturday as he went off again and broke the back part of the undertray. It was a fight against time to get his car ready for qualifying. Five minutes before the session started, though, the floor was finished. It worked as Schumacher managed to split the two McLarens, which meant that the grid line up for Sunday would be Hakkinen on pole, Schumacher second, Coulthard third and Irvine fourth. The scene was set for another Ferrari victory.

The first start to the race was immediately aborted because Jos Verstappen had remained motionless on the grid. But in the second start, Schumacher pulled ahead of Hakkinen with Irvine roaring into second place. And that's exactly how the race finished: a one-two for Ferrari and the

SCHUMACHER ON THE ROAD

Although Bruno Romani and Claudio Degli Espositi cook for the entire Ferrari team when it is away from home, Michael Schumacher's personal fitness guru, Indian maestro Balbir Singh is the one responsible for supervising the German's meals.

Claudio comments, 'Mr Singh prepares Schumacher's lunch at mid-day. He usually has boiled rice and a selection of vegetables, such as onions, broccoli, carrots and beans. It's a bit of a stir fry with soy sauce added – and a dash of curry powder, of course. On one occasion I remember, Schumacher wasn't very well, so he asked for a special lunch; he had a different combination of vegetables but still had curry powder.'

Despite his reservations about the wisdom of using curry powder as a cure for an upset stomach, Claudio admires the Schumacher balance of eating and driving. 'Schumacher is fast on the track and slow at eating. It's the ideal combination for him and the team.'

Singh is also on hand to give Schumacher any massages that he requires before or after the races or practice sessions.

Michael isn't the type of driver who just turns up for the races, then goes home again. He likes to be in the team environment, but he also realizes that he can't be everywhere at once, and therefore only appears at official FIA press conferences to talk about what's happening at the track rather than giving one-to-one interviews with individual members of the press. He needs to stay focused on the job – and that is to win races.

whole of Italy exploded with joy.

Ferrari Chairman Luca di Montezemolo met the team at Bologna airport on Sunday night. He was overjoyed. 'This is a great victory which rewards everyone at Ferrari for putting both cars at the head of the field and keeping them there to the finish. This win is also a reward for Goodyear, without whose technical steps forward, this result would not have been possible.'

Jean Todt, the courageous Frenchman who has led his team into battle and built up what is now a Championship competing team, was rewarded with the one-two victory, which occurred on the fifth anniversary of his arrival at Ferrari. Was it a prophesy of things to come? Schumacher was hopeful but kept everyone's feet firmly on the ground: 'I was sure we would have beaten McLaren at some point, although I didn't expect it to be quite so decisive. It's down to the fact that we've chosen the right route from a technical point of view. It's impossible to separate things, but overall the car is better and faster, in practice and in the race.'

There were still improvements to achieve. Schumacher wanted more from the aerodynamics and a little more from the tyres. Next stop was Silverstone, which Schumacher expected to be completely different. 'Without doubt the track at Silverstone has different characteristics to the one at Magny-Cours. We also need different tyres, ones that are adapted to the race. But we should be able to compete with McLaren's one or two tenths' advantage. This victory is much more important than the previous ones. In Argentina the conditions favoured us, and in Canada the McLarens had problems, but here we beat them. The modifications we had on the car worked fantastically well and considering that we have more coming along, then I believe I have a Ferrari that can really take me to the top.'

IRVINE KEEPS UP
HE STAYS A CLOSE SECOND TO MICHAEL

Eddie Irvine was also demonstrating that he was not far behind the man that many regard as the greatest driver of his generation. His qualifying ability had improved and he had driven a great race to hang on to second place. It was a good moment for Irvine to demonstrate his prowess as his contract was under discussion. He had kept Hakkinen at bay and that was important for the team. As Irvine said, 'Obviously, I thought Hakkinen could get second place, but I was quite calm as he knows how difficult it is to pass me, and he also knew it wasn't worth taking risks. However, I didn't have any particular problems; this Ferrari has confirmed that it's very strong and Michael can battle for the Championship.'

● ● ●

Silverstone was about to surprise the Ferraris. It had never been a lucky track for either Schumacher or Irvine. In fact, for Irvine it had always been somewhat of a nightmare. Now a combination of factors was about to turn the situation around and victory was close once again.

CHAPTER THIRTEEN

Mid-Season Blues

'If you are battling wheel to wheel with another guy, it can often end in tears.'

Ross Brawn

Half-way through the season, the Formula One playroom was once more alive with bitching and sniping and, as usual, head boy Michael Schumacher was at the centre of it all. Heinz-Harald Frentzen was still unamused at being unceremoniously woken up as he trudged around the track in Montreal, and Jacques Villeneuve had decided to join those pointing the finger to complain about Schumacher's behaviour.

Several drivers were saying Schumacher was unfit to be a director of the Drivers' Trade Union (the GPDA), but Schumacher was unmoved. 'I don't want to kill anyone. I don't hate anyone. I'm not in love with them, they're not my friends, but I don't have a particular problem. If we weren't racers we would have a good time, but we *are* racers and we fight hard so it's difficult to get on. I'm sick of Frentzen's complaints. I've said many times I didn't see him. I'm not so stupid as to risk a victory by collision. The GPDA is a democratic organization, the directors [currently David Coulthard, Damon Hill and Schumacher himself] are elected by all the members, so if Frentzen wants me out, he can put it on the minutes of the next meeting, then the majority can decide.'

The constant whingeing of the other drivers is not something that surprises Ferrari's technical director, Ross Brawn: 'I find there are generally three categories of people who have a view about Michael. The first category consists of people who really know him, and a very high proportion of them have a very good opinion of him. If you talk to the people at Benetton and Ferrari about Michael, they all like him and get on with him. The second category consists of people who know Michael but resent his ability. These people are mainly other racing drivers who know that in a straight race he'd just thrash them every weekend, and they are jealous of that fact. The third category consists of people who do not know Michael and just form their opinions from the media. He doesn't go out of his way to change people's opinions of him.'

Brawn thinks the very competitive nature of F1 precludes the kind of matey behaviour found in other sports. 'If you are battling wheel to wheel with another guy it can often end in tears. One comes off worse and whinges. I defy anyone to handle it better than Michael in such a competitive environment.'

And so there is a kind of stand-off situation – the second raters against the man who, if they were all in the same cars, would win consistently week after week. Could Schumi ever see himself going off on a lads' holiday with, say, Damon Hill and Jacques Villeneuve? He looks perplexed, then grins: 'I'd take them to that place you go once and then never go back. I suppose it depends on the circumstances but I don't know what we'd talk about. Quite frankly, I'd rather spend time with my family.'

Irvine and Schumacher may not have similar lifestyles, but they are both passionate about racing, and Silverstone was fast approaching. Although he hasn't had a lot of success there, it is a circuit that Schumacher respects. As he says, 'It's very challenging; a driver can make a difference as there are a lot of high speed corners.'

After two victories so far in the 1998 season, it would be nice to make it a hat-trick. And as Italy and Germany were both out of the World Cup it was up to Ferrari to provide the glamour and excitement in sport.

THE SILVERSTONE AFFAIR
A VICTORY MARKED BY CONTROVERSY

Although Hakkinen qualified in pole position at Silverstone, Schumacher was in second place on the grid with Coulthard fourth and Irvine fifth. The scene was set for another

McLaren/Ferrari battle royal. The 90,000-plus fans, who braved the appalling weather, were rewarded with a race full of incidents and a finish that saw the rainbow of luck bless Schumacher the victor and Irvine, who was on the podium in third place.

But like other occasions, Schumacher's victory was marked by controversy. On lap 40 Coulthard spun out of the race, handing Schumacher second position. Hakkinen was still leading when the pouring rain and dangerous driving conditions, which had already accounted for numerous cars spinning off, saw the Safety Car come out on lap 44 for five laps. Naturally, Schumacher was able to close the gap between himself and Hakkinen, and by lap 51, the German genuinely had Hakkinen under pressure and, hey presto! the Finn spun over the grass before rejoining the race.

Schumacher was in the lead, but it wasn't all over. Ferrari team manager Stefano Domenicali had been handed a document from the stewards stating that Michael Schumacher had infringed a rule and had to be brought in to the pits for a 10-second penalty.

Confusion. As Stefano says, 'I was completely perplexed by it. I read it two or three times and still didn't understand it. The problem was that the important part of the communication [the part that states which article it was relating to] was hand-written so we couldn't tell if it was referring to Article 56c or 56e.

'There were only two or three laps to go, the stewards' room was a long way from the pits plus, and to make it even worse, our radio communication with Michael wasn't working. But a decision had to be made. We brought Michael in on the last lap, thus conforming clearly with the regulation allowing you to make the stop within three laps of its notification. I know the rules and regulations inside out. If I didn't know them I'd be out of a job, and I knew this decision was not right.'

Eddie Irvine did a great job that afternoon and ended the race an excellent third. It was all the more remarkable considering that he had slipped from fifth to 11th at the start.

After Canada and France, yet another new front wing was produced for Silverstone, leading to yet another Ferrari victory. But for Ferrari team boss Jean Todt the celebrations were far from over. Straight after the race at Silverstone he flew to Paris to watch the World Cup final between France and Brazil, which was won by France.

After Silverstone the two Ferrari drivers re-signed for the stable of the prancing horse. Schumi is now tied to Ferrari until the end of 2002 for a reputed £20 million a year. With sponsorship deals this could earn him as much as £175 million. But he denied that his motivation for re-signing was financial. 'I've had some financial proposals which are similar, and in some cases superior, to that of Ferrari, but there are some arguments which are more important than economic ones. For example, the immense amount of work the team has undertaken and the continued support I have received in my years at Maranello were instrumental in me not looking at other possibilities.'

A couple of weeks later, Eddie Irvine also re-signed for the Scuderia for another year for a reputed £3.5 million. Although it was rumoured he might go to Williams, he decided in the end that being Number Two to Schumacher was better than being Number One in a less competitive team. There was always the dream of victory, and one day it would come.

Next stop, Austria. But would Ferrari's winning streak

continue? After the euphoria of Canada, France and Britain, the team was about to receive a cold shower, colder in terms of reducing morale than all the rain at Silverstone.

Qualifying was a strange affair. The fans used to seeing the silver arrows of McLaren compete for the front row with the passionate red of Ferrari, were in for a surprise when Benetton's Giancarlo Fisichella qualified in pole position, with Jean Alesi's Sauber second. Hakkinen was third with Michael Schumacher fourth, Eddie Irvine eighth and Coulthard way back in 14th place.

It looked as though there might be a surprise victor, but no, Hakkinen was the winner, after an excellent start. And it was, in fact, Hakkinen's turn to get his own back on Schumacher for depriving him of victory at Silverstone. For once, the Finn forced the German to make an error. On lap 17 Schumacher went off in spectacular fashion damaging his nose cone, but somehow hanging onto the car. He went into the pits on lap 18 to have a new nose fitted and re-joined the race in 16th place.

With the pit stops complete, Irvine was placed third, with Schumacher directly behind him in fourth. But Michael desperately needed the points, so on lap 68 he passed his team-mate who was supposedly fighting brake problems. Some wit actually asked Jean Todt at the end of the race, 'And when did you decide that Irvine had brake problems?' But the team kept a straight face and the Camp Commandant, Bernie Ecclestone, gave them the benediction of his observation that 'Schumacher's car was faster than Irvine's, so it was logical that he should pass him'.

As Jean Todt said, 'In order to fight for first place, Michael, who was on a two-stop strategy, absolutely had to pass Hakkinen and so he was driving right on the limit. The car was damaged when he went off and was repaired in the pits. He then climbed up through the field from last place to get onto the podium. After a good start, Eddie drove an attacking race. He had brake problems in the final stages and we warned him of this. For that reason, he did not take any unnecessary risks in keeping his team-mate behind him. The Championship is still very open and we have picked up seven points. We know our main opposition is very strong, but we will not give up the fight.'

Schumacher remained bullish: 'I made a risky aerodynamic choice and I paid for it. If I'd started in the lead I would have won.' He was also quick to silence the voices that tried to make a meal out of Irvine's relinquished third place. 'The way in which McLaren behaved at the first race [Coulthard's obvious manoeuvre to let Hakkinen past to take victory after their pre-race agreement] was ridiculous. From the other side, it is normal that my team would try not to make my life difficult during the race, and that Irvine, seeing me near him, would let me pass, without making it as obvious as Coulthard did with Hakkinen in Melbourne.'

There were also harsh words from the double World Champion about the paddock rumours that Ferrari had not gone well due to the fact that something illegal had been taken off the car after Silverstone (supposedly a system of traction control). 'The people who say these things should make an official protest. I never accuse anyone of cheating. There are official channels which can clarify the situation. The stewards came to our garage and checked the car from top to bottom and found everything was all right. This leaves me to tell these people who accuse us of cheating to shut up.'

Ferrari's technical director, Ross Brawn, was more circumspect, but as adamant as Schumacher on the cheating question: 'I'm afraid it's perennial in Formula One. There is always the perception that Ferrari gets special treatment and gets away with much more than the other teams. I worked at Benetton when there was a belief there that Ferrari was getting favoured team status. Having worked at Ferrari I can assure you it's not true.'

Yet Bernie Ecclestone goes out of his way to say how much he wants Ferrari to win. Brawn thinks this is natural. 'Bernie's being truthful. From a commercial point of view it is better for Ferrari to win the Championship. Ferrari has the largest fan club, an international following, a German driver, an Italian team. We are the biggest team in Formula One. Nobody can be stupid or naive enough not to accept that it will do Formula One more good if Ferrari wins rather than McLaren, but that doesn't mean anyone is trying to manipulate the situation.

'I know Ron [Dennis, McLaren's team boss] has commented that he doesn't think it's quite a level playing field. I've seen both sides of it and I think it's pretty even. Sometimes it runs for you. Sometimes it doesn't.'

STRATEGY COUNTS
A MASTER LESSON FROM ROSS BRAWN

Schumacher's home race at Hockenheim in Germany was not the place to be off the pace. But that's just what happened. Schumacher was nearly a second behind Hakkinen after the Friday practice session. Qualifying was disastrous. He was 1.5 seconds slower than pole man Hakkinen, and consequently down the grid in ninth position. For once Irvine out qualified his team-mate and ended up in sixth.

The new long wheel base was used for the race, together

with another front wing that was suited to high-speed races. But it was not going to change the outcome of a difficult weekend. At the start Eddie maintained his grid position and Michael moved into eighth, then seventh on the first lap. Having overtaking his team-mate, then making his only pit stop on lap 24 (Eddie pitted on the following lap) he kept his sixth position to the end. Meanwhile, Irvine dropped to eighth because of a longer pit stop. It was not a good day.

Jean Todt said: 'Today's race reflected our performance throughout the weekend. We knew that overtaking, when the cars had pretty much the same performance level, was going to be almost impossible. Michael made up two places on the first lap and a further one with his pit stop. Because Eddie slightly overshot his pit stop position, he lost a couple of seconds which cost him two places. Our car was not up to the performance level of our closest rivals, as we have seen over the past three days.'

And on to Hungary. Yet nothing had changed in the interim two weeks. Hakkinen qualified on pole, Coulthard second, Michael Schumacher third, Eddie in fifth place. It looked like the McLaren superiority had re-appeared and the rest of the season was just going to be a procession of McLaren wins. But Ferrari's master strategist Ross Brawn was about to give the world another lesson in how races can still be won with cunning and attention to detail.

On lap 13 Irvine retired with gearbox problems, but Schumacher remained third behind the McLarens. On lap 43 the German made his second stop and the McLarens fell into the trap by following the Ferrari. Coulthard made his second pit stop on lap 44 and Hakkinen on lap 46. Schumacher was now in the lead, but what McLaren didn't know was that he was on a three-stop strategy. Schumacher just had to build a lead of around 30 seconds to make sure he would still be leading when he came out from his third pit stop. After a heart-stopping moment on lap 52 when he went off the track, but managed to get back with the engine still running, he was off into the distance. On lap 62 he made his last pit stop and came out ahead of Coulthard and McLaren team-mate Hakkinen, who was having mechanical problems. Game, set and match to Ferrari.

Ross Brawn made it look easy. 'Quite frankly, we had nothing to lose. The guy in fourth place was so far behind it wasn't significant, so the worst we could do was finish third. Hungary is sensitive to tyre decay, and sensitive to fuel weight. That, combined with a couple of other things, makes it perfect for a three-stop strategy. We just went for it.'

Ferrari is a team that loves the cut and thrust of winning and losing in the pit lane. As Ross Brawn says, 'I enjoy it. I think it's a very rewarding part of the job when you get it right. Some people don't seem to relish it but from Ferrari's point of view we all enjoy that side of things and I think we get it right more often than we get it wrong.'

So off to Spa, Schumacher's favourite circuit. He was aiming for his fourth consecutive win there, and with heavy rain forecast for race day it looked like his dreams would come true. But reality can sometimes be somewhat different to fantasy.

The first indication that this wasn't going to be Ferrari's weekend was apparent in the qualifying session: Hakkinen on pole, Coulthard second, Schumacher and Irvine fourth and fifth, with Damon Hill an unexpected third.

The race started with a massive 12-car pile up after Coulthard lost control of his McLaren. Although Irvine was involved, Schumacher wasn't, so the Irishman was given the spare car for the re-start. At the second start, Michael went into second place and Eddie third. Hakkinen was out immediately after he and Schumacher managed to touch cars at the start, and the Finn was then hit by Johnny Herbert in his Sauber.

On lap 11, Michael passed Damon Hill to take the lead (although Hill was to be the eventual winner) and things were going to plan. Then, tragedy. On lap 26, with visibility down to zero, and the rain driving across the track, Schumi came across Coulthard, who had managed to take the re-start. Despite the fact the double World Champion had been trying to overtake the Scot for the last two laps, Coulthard had not budged from his racing line; then he decided to let Schumacher pass, but it was too little too late. Schumacher smacked straight into the back of the McLaren forcing the retirement of both cars. The German drove back to the pits on three wheels, climbed out of his car and stormed off towards the McLaren garage.

Team Manager Stefano Domenicali tried desperately to stop Schumacher, but the man was not for turning. He wanted justice and he was going to get it. Coulthard, with his helmet still on, was protected by his mechanics and Schumacher only got as far as screaming 'Why did you try and kill me?' before he was led away by Jean Todt, Domenicali, Claudio Berro, Pino Gozzo and other team members. Ten points down the drain, the World Championship lying in tatters... it was Ferrari's worst day of the season. Schumacher was distraught.

Domenicali was at the centre of the storm but there was nothing he could do. 'When I turned round on the pit wall, I saw Michael heading for the McLaren garage. I immediately ran up to him and tried to convince him not to do anything stupid, but he was too concentrated to listen. I am generally a very calm person so I try to transmit this to all the team. They were all quite nervous.'

When the dust had settled, the facts emerged. Coulthard had not braked but neither had he accelerated out of the corner, so Schumacher ran into him. Everyone had their views on the subject. Irvine said, 'DC should have let him through a lot earlier. What DC was playing at I don't know. He had a lot of corners to let Michael through. Okay, I don't think what he did was deliberate, but it wasn't a good piece of driving, and it wasn't a good piece of stewarding either, because he held Michael up for too long. He should have pulled into the pits and been given a 10-second penalty, or given a penalty after the race for holding up the leader that long. It was totally out of order. On the other hand, Michael was 35 seconds up the road; there was no need for him to be in such a hurry.'

The other aspect that surprised Irvine was that Schumacher drove the car back to the pits. It should have been undrivable. 'I was surprised he drove back to the pits as it was quite dangerous.' Danger wasn't on Schumacher's mind. As he said, 'I really wanted to finish the race; if I could have done it on three wheels I would have.'

But the controversy didn't stop there. Even within the team there were those who thought that Coulthard had made a huge mistake and should be punished, and those who thought he had made a huge mistake but that Schumacher shouldn't have been so close. The truth is hard to ascertain. Schumacher is without doubt the greatest driver of his generation and perhaps beyond, but he is human. Did he make an error?

Nigel Stepney was also in two minds about it all. 'At Spa we were in a position of being able to finish 1 and 2 and in the end we had zero points. Michael had an unfortunate incident with Coulthard. It's easy to look back now, but we can't do anything about it, so it's best forgetten. We learnt from it.'

What? He laughed, then went on to provide a deep insight into the abilities of the great drivers. 'Drivers drive at 100 per cent, and when they're told to slow down very few of them can slow down and take it easy. Ayrton Senna was leading by miles in Monaco one year, and when he was told to slow down he crashed. He stopped pushing, started to take it easy but lost concentration. When that happens your points of reference change. Every driver has to find his own way of taking it easy. Some reduce the revs but still maintain 100 per cent concentration; they just use the engine less.

'In Hungary when Michael was told to slow down he went faster. I'm not criticizing Michael; without him we wouldn't be where we are today, we wouldn't have the high calibre of people working for us and we wouldn't be in the position we are in. But he was well ahead of everybody...'

Schumacher has his own point of view. 'In Spa I wasn't totally on the limit. In Hungary I took it easy and was about a second a lap slower. If I can go slowly I will. The most difficult thing is getting the last 5 per cent out of the car. You can get to 95 per cent but that last 5 per cent is always difficult to find. You have to work proportionally a lot harder.'

For Ross Brawn, Spa was the low point of the season. 'It was a real tragedy, especially as we end the season in a situation where Spa would have been significant. I don't think Coulthard did it on purpose. But I don't think he did a very smart thing and I also resent the fact that for a lap he was very conscious that Michael was there and just made life difficult for him. Going through the hairpin at the end of the pit straight Michael clearly had the easy line to overtake him, but Coulthard blocked him.

STEFANO DOMENICALI

Stefano Domenicali is the youngest senior manager at Ferrari. Bright and enthusiastic by nature, he is in charge of personnel, as well as the Mugello race track.

Bearing in mind the pressure on Ferrari from the outside world, it is a difficult and demanding job. It is made more complex by the fact that Ferrari, unlike the other Formula One teams, is not a standalone operation; it also produces high-performance road cars, and this means that the two areas must be in harmony from the point of view of structure and organization. As Domenicali says, 'The fundamental thing is that our strategy for our Sports Department fits into the overall strategy of Ferrari. It is vital we have one united image.'

Domenicali may be young, but he has the maturity to withstand the tempests caused by problems and place a steady hand on the tiller so that explosive situations between personnel are avoided.

He is also building for the future. 'We are one of the youngest teams in Formula One. In the short term, difficulties arise due to lack of experience, but we have huge potential. We are investing long term and we must look to the future in a logical and calm manner.'

Domenicali's job is to manage and talk to people. 'Every person needs to be managed differently. Understanding people and their various needs is very interesting and stimulating work. Some have difficult and complex characters and I have to act as a negatiator and smooth things over. The best way [to solve problems] is to sit down and talk, but sometimes we also have to remind people of their responsibilities.'

'Unfortunately, there was a background to it all and Coulthard has said before and since that he is still upset by what Michael did to him in Argentina. We believe Coulthard had been told by his team that Michael was there so he can't claim any ignorance of the fact Michael was behind him. Suddenly he made the decision to let Michael pass after giving him some aggravation. Technically, he didn't accelerate out of the corner which in those conditions was as good as lifting off, so we had the incident. The end result was that what should have been a fairly straightforward win for Michael didn't happen.'

Brawn understands Michael's reaction even if he doesn't agree with it. 'I've never seen him as cross as that. I think it probably took him a week to calm down. I can understand it; at that stage of the race he would have thought it was in the bag and would have been counting the points. He went into the McLaren garage convinced that Coulthard had deliberately tried to put him out of the race. I understand why he thought that, although I can't condone what he did because it's not good. But I defy anyone else in similar circumstances to behave any differently.'

What about the race debrief? Ross Brawn laughs. 'We didn't have one that day; it was best to just let things calm down.'

Nigel Stepney said, 'The drivers get very stressed in the car; there's so much adrenaline running they can't control it. It's happened to a lot of drivers; they end up with people hanging onto them to try and stop them doing something stupid.'

For Jean Todt, Spa was a positive experience. 'It made us even stronger as a team, as Michael realized that the team was supporting him. The best way to get over Spa was to stay together.'

The last word goes to Michael Schumacher: 'Spa was the lowest point of the season. I've never felt so many negative emotions which I expressed immediately after the race. It's fairly natural when you feel you've been thrown out of the race by someone who's not competing for first place. I'm not someone who goes to hit a fellow driver, I just wanted to talk. When he [Coulthard] came out of the corner he didn't accelerate normally. He tried to let me pass, but he did it in a not very professional way. Instead of approaching the next corner and staying on the side and giving me the racing line, he slowed down in the middle of the straight. You just don't have the chance to see how much distance you have between you and the person in front. Whoever thought I should have left more gap is wrong, as I would have crashed into him anyway.'

● ● ●

The roller-coaster ride of ups and downs continued. Germany was a disaster. Hungary was victory. Spa a disaster. And Monza was a victory in the most unexpected way.

CHAPTER FOURTEEN

An Upturn in Fortunes

*'I know how hard everyone has been
working at Maranello. It might be
old fashioned, but hard work always
pays, even in modern times.'*

Fiat Boss Gianni Agnelli
after the victory at Monza

Monza. The home ground of the famous *tifosi*. After Spa there was tension between Coulthard and Schumacher and so a meeting was staged for the two to discuss their differences. It took place on neutral ground in the Winfield motorhome and lasted one-and-a-half hours. The content of the conversations was kept secret, but when they emerged from the meeting, the two shook hands for the photographers and the situation was defused. Another racing accident. Now it was time to concentrate on Monza, the 600th Grand Prix for Ferrari.

The first indication that this weekend would be special came when Schumacher got his first pole position of the year. Irvine, meanwhile, was fifth. Although Sylvester Stallone, Mick Jagger and a host of stars graced the Italian circuit with their presence, the real star of the show was the red F300, which the *tifosi* were willing to victory.

The start was disastrous for the Ferraris, both of which were overtaken by the McLarens to leave Eddie in third position and Michael fifth. But by the time the leaders had all completed their pit stops, Michael was first and Eddie third. On lap 49 Eddie passed Hakkinen and after 53 laps, the two Ferraris took the chequered flag in first and second place.

Delirium all round. As Edward Asprey said: 'I thought I was going to be hurled to the ground in the pit lane after the victory. It was the most emotional day of my three years with Ferrari. To see the fans hysterical with joy was fantastic. It was just a stunning victory. One-two at Monza has to be the dream of everyone involved with Ferrari. It is a day I will never forget.'

There was double joy for Schumacher; not only was his team-mate second but brother Ralf was third, the first time the Schumacher brothers had been on the podium together. Michael was overjoyed: 'Without doubt I needed to win here to cancel out the disappointment of Spa. I know that a lot of fans were very down after Belgium and I needed to fight back.' Ferrari was back in with a chance of the World Championship. Now Hakkinen (who finished fourth at Monza) and Schumacher were neck and neck on 80 points each. There was everything to play for at the Nurburgring and Suzuka, and Schumacher was in a confident mood. 'I'm looking forward to the Nurburgring because I thought Monza would be harder for the Ferraris than the Nurburgring, which should be good for us.'

Monza is a fast circuit, usually not so suited to the Ferraris, but the V10 engine had proved that the Scuderia could compete with anyone on circuits that depend on engine power as well as driver ability.

Paolo Martinelli has been pleased with the development of the Ferrari V10 engine this year. 'Apart from Australia when the engine blew up for a very banal reason, the V10 has gone exceptionally well. For Spa and Monza we made another step; together with Shell we have developed a winning combination. We have had excellent feedback from the drivers on the drivability, reliability and power of the 047 V10 engine. Shell has given us a fuel that has significantly increased the horsepower of the engine as it allows us to realise its full potential in another place'.

Shell's support has been vital for the team this year. Ross Brawn is adamant that without it, Ferrari would not have been able to make the technological progress it has. 'Shell is a dedicated partner in every area. We wouldn't enjoy the high level of reliability we have without the support of Shell. The trackside support is vital. We now have an analysis system for the fuel that is the same as FIA's, and this means we can constantly check and control that the fuel is legal at all times. Extreme weather conditions like heat or an accidental mix of

THE FACTORY AT FIORANO

If you walk around the Formula One factory next to the test track at Fiorano, one thing that strikes you is the cleanliness; everything is spotless, even the huge engine assembly room, where after each race the engines are taken apart and studied. In the main plant area you are surrounded by history; you can almost feel the presence of the Commendatore, Enzo Ferrari and imagine him strolling round the factory checking on his men and his cars. From Giorgio Ascanelli's office there is a bird's eye view of the factory floor and the three bays where the mechanics work on the cars. By opening the large window Ascanelli can appear, like Mussolini on his balcony, and dictate the state of play. A large open-plan drawing office furnished with the latest computer equipment and offices at the side for the chiefs, brings that part of the building into the 20th Century. One is constantly reminded that Ferrari is more than just a Formula One team.

The magical moment is when you walk round the corner from the mechanical parts section and gaze on rows of new road cars, each waiting to be hand finished. Each car has a note attached to it specifying its country of destination, the type of car, the colour of the bodywork and the internal colours. Here is the dream centre, the big boys' playroom, the place where only the chosen few, clients and VIPs to be precise, are allowed to wander.

fuels can make the fuel illegal, but we have the peace of mind of knowing that we are always within the legal limits.

'The lubricants are like blood, and the fuel food, so it is good for us to be able to check that all our components are in optimum working order. I cannot imagine Ferrari without Shell, or indeed Formula One without Shell. It has made a contribution of enormous proportions to our success over the last three years.' Simon Dunning of Shell is proud that it has managed to use its experience with Ferrari to create products for road cars. 'The Shell Ultra Helix X that you put in your car is a direct result of our work with Ferrari.'

Two races remained and everything looked like it was going Ferrari's way, but in Formula One there's no such thing as a dead certainty.

THE LAST EUROPEAN RACE
THE FERRARI CAMP WERE CONFIDENT

Bernie Ecclestone has succeeded where others have failed; he has made Germany a part of Luxembourg. The Nurburgring, for the purpose of the sponsors (most notably the cigarette sponsors) is, for a few days of the year, part of Luxembourg. That way teams can carry the names of the cigarette companies on their livery.

Going to the Nurburgring, the Ferrari camp were positive about their chances of winning, even more so after Schumacher qualified in pole position and Irvine second. It all seemed set for another stupendous victory. After the win at Monza, Fiat boss Gianni Agnelli was moved to comment, 'I know how hard everyone has been working at Maranello. It might be old fashioned, but hard work always pays, even in modern times. Luca [di Montezemolo, the Ferrari chairman] is a great worker, who is leading Ferrari in the right direction. Monza was a great example of man and machine working in perfect harmony.'

With both Ferraris on the front row, victory should have been a formality, but it looked as if Schumacher and Irvine had different cars to the ones they had used in qualifying, and in effect that is what they had.

After a great start with Eddie leading Michael, the Ferraris quickly went off the boil. The tyres, particularly the front ones, were wearing quickly. Schumacher made his first pit stop on lap 24 but as Ross Brawn says, 'Michael was on the radio calling for new tyres from about lap 20. Our plan was to go on much longer than that. For once it didn't come together for us.'

The race finished with Hakkinen winning, Schumacher second and Coulthard third. Hakkinen was now four points ahead of Schumacher, and there was just one race to go.

Hakkinen had been able to pass Irvine during the race, and some people thought the Irishman had not made it difficult enough for the Finn. But he is clear about what happened: 'Everyone's saying, how wonderful, the McLarens had an amazing strategy at the Nurburgring. That's just bullshit. The McLaren was a second a lap quicker; it's very hard to f**k up when the car's a second a lap quicker. I was driving my own race. He [Hakkinen] got past me. He was over a second a lap faster than me at the time. I couldn't hold him up. I can't be blamed for Michael not winning the race. When has that ever happened? When has a driver been blamed for his team-mate not winning a race? It's so ridiculous, it's unbelievable. It would have been nice if I could have held on a little longer, but I don't think we should be relying on me holding up another driver so the Number One can win the race. The problem at the Nurburgring was that we weren't quick enough.'

Ross Brawn was also a supporter of Irvine against Hakkinen. 'It's easy to judge from the outside. Everyone was disappointed that Hakkinen overtook Eddie, but what could he or should he have done? If he'd hit Hakkinen there would have been a huge outcry. We certainly don't want the Championship ending with the controversies we had last year. Hakkinen managed to get a run at Eddie. By the time Eddie realized what was happening there were two options: one was to play it straight and let him past, and the other was to try and knock him off the track, which isn't the proper way of doing things. He didn't really have much choice.

'The race at the Nurburgring didn't evolve very well for us. For once the track conditions worked against us. Sunday turned out to be particularly cold and we couldn't get the car to handle or the tyres to work. This was a race when neither McLaren driver made a mistake; they applied a good strategy which we couldn't beat. They made two pit stops at exactly the right time and they responded correctly to what we tried to do with Michael. We just weren't able to beat them.'

THE FINAL COUNTDOWN
DOWN TO THE WIRE AGAIN

Suzuka. The last race of the season. There was everything to play for and, with five weeks since the Luxembourg Grand Prix, an unusually long time to prepare for it. But still this wasn't long enough. The activity at Maranello was frantic. Immediately after the Nurburgring the team went to Barcelona to test, but Eddie Irvine was missing. His back was playing up again. The week after, at the beginning of October, the team returned to base, and both Schumacher and Irvine tested the car at Fiorano. The pressure was on, and most of it was aimed at Eddie Irvine. Schumacher, superstar and double World Champion, was used to the burden of being Number One, and to compensate for the pressure he also has the exceptional experience that comes from being a champion.

Irvine is a very good driver and an excellent team-mate but he had never been expected to be Schumacher. As he says,

'Everyone thinks he [Schumacher] is good, but they don't seem to realize just how good he is. It is down to pure driving ability. No one gets near it and I don't know anyone who's ever got near it. Mika's a nice guy but he's not in the same class. I have to say that Michael's at least as good as Senna, and you have to look at what Senna did to Hakkinen in the same car, he nearly lapped him. Michael seems to be the only guy who can get the maximum out of the car, whether it's difficult or not, which is a bit of a downer for the rest of us as he makes us look silly.'

And what about Suzuka? 'Well for a start, you don't have to brake too much so it's better for my back,' says Irvine. Unfortunately, as Rory Byrne says, Eddie is not aerodynamically suited to racing. His body is long and his legs are proportionally shorter making it almost impossible for him to be comfortable. But that doesn't mean he can't be fast. This has been his best year so far — seven podiums and fourth overall in the Drivers' Championship.

However, that is not enough. Irvine is as dedicated and ambitious as Schumacher. Without Schumacher he would also have had his first win by now. He was leading by a distance last year in Suzuka, before he had to give way to Schumi, who was going for the title. This year could be more of the same. Does he feel under pressure?

'Not really. I do my own job, that's all I can do. I can't be blamed for someone else not winning the Championship. I can only do my best. It's been this situation all year; we've performed to a certain level and now all of a sudden we're not going to change things overnight. We can do our best, but if McLaren are faster...

'Our reliability and strategy, and the fact that the two drivers are very well suited are our strong points. The car's not fast enough, we know that. But for our situation, Suzuka is the best track to have the last race. Both Michael and I go well there. We've always done so. We just have to qualify well. I have to be on the front row or the second row. If not, there's not a lot I can do.'

Nigel Stepney has some encouraging words about the Irishman: 'Eddie has come on a lot this year. He's had more kilometres testing and the car is more to his liking. He's a very good second driver to Michael. It's important when testing to have a driver who is able to drive almost like Michael. About 99 per cent of the time when we test with Eddie we can use the same data for Michael. Two drivers who understand each other make a stronger team; they need to be compatible. We are testing almost every day until we go to Japan – the engine, the tyres, the chassis ... we can't do a lot more than we're doing. If you have a chance of going for the Championship you give it 100 per cent.'

But there is no doubt that Eddie is under more pressure than ever before. Before departing for Japan Stefano Domenicali said, 'We are going to Japan knowing we have to do our best. There must be no excuses. We have to have a really good race with both drivers. He [Eddie] realizes that he has to do something that is very important for the team and also for himself. He has to show everyone that he has had a good season, and he has to finish the season with the best race performance of his career. He realizes that. Everyone knows what they have to do.'

Ferrari expect a lot, but to compensate for the pressure they give Eddie his own back-up team. Domenicali continued, 'We try to do our best by spending time on the seat problem. Yesterday, we spent all day trying to find a solution. This morning we have also been working on the problem. We want to give him the optimum conditions for the last race. Sonia [his sister and physio] will be with him, and so will Fred [the team doctor] who will concentrate on him and make sure he is ready for the race.'

Ross Brawn also made it clear that the Eddie factor would be vital: 'The added complication of Suzuka is that it's not good enough for Michael to finish first and Mika second. We have to ensure that Eddie plays a role, more so this weekend than at any race this year, and so our thinking will revolve around that as well. And I'm sure McLaren are also thinking of how Coulthard can play a role in the whole equation. We have got a situation where we have nothing to lose. Therefore, in some ways it's easier for us than it is for them. They've got to adopt a slightly more conservative approach. We know we have to beat them or else we can't win the Championship. We will be going all out to win it. Unless we have an attacking approach to the weekend we're not going to achieve our victory goal, so we may as well go for it and see what happens.'

Everyone in the team was highly motivated. In addition there was still some bad blood between Ferrari and McLaren over the various on-track incidents, the most obvious being Spa, which could cost Ferrari the Championship. But Brawn didn't see this as a problem. 'Those things (like Spa) happen. Something similar may happen to Hakkinen in Japan. Maybe there'll be a set of circumstances where he comes off worse in a similar incident. They've all got a habit of balancing themselves over a reasonable enough period. I think that will be the case in Japan.'

Ferrari were certainly not going to be intimidated by anything McLaren may choose to throw at them. As Domenicali said, 'Ron Dennis is fighting his battle. They can fight for the title in various ways, technical, political, psychological, but we will not fall into the trap.'

The dream was still to win the Drivers' and Constructors' Championships. Even though the Constructors' was almost out of reach, Nigel Stepney was not giving up. 'We haven't lost the Constructors' Championship yet. If we win 1 and 2 and McLaren don't get any points, we've won it. The door's still open.' And while the door's still open, there's hope. Stepney wants to win, but he also has his dream. 'My dream would be for Eddie to win the race, Michael second and Hakkinen out. We really want Eddie to win. He deserves it.'

It was apparent that Eddie now had a great deal of respect from the team. Schumacher's race engineer, Ignazio Lunetta says, 'This year Eddie is more motivated, he has more faith. He is really part of the team and he has more confidence in us, and we in him. He's less of a playboy and more serious. And we think more of him.'

When Schumacher arrived in Italy to resume testing, all the bosses were present to hover attentively on the sidelines. Goodyear Team Boss, Perry Bell was on hand to react to feedback on the tyres. A large Goodyear truck was parked by the side of the press centre. Goodyear might be leaving Formula One but it is as committed as ever; in fact it couldn't be more committed, even if it were staying.

Ross Brawn is impressed with Goodyear and immensely sad that the American company is pulling out of Formula One. 'If we could stay with Goodyear, I'd be confident in predicting that from the first race next year we'd be very competitive. They have done an excellent job this year. We've really started to get rolling and now they've withdrawn, which is a terrible shame. It's very unfortunate, as our technical relationship with Goodyear has developed and expanded enormously. It's now a much stronger partnership and it's a shame that it is coming to an end as both teams have seen what the partnership is capable of doing. Goodyear are totally committed to winning the Championship and will be with us right until the end.'

Jean Todt and Ross Brawn popped by to see Schumacher and catch up on the morning's testing. Then at 1 pm precisely,

Schumi entered the press room-cum-restaurant for his lunch. Immediately afterwards it was back to testing. The media were getting restless, and after an hour there was another break and a round of television interviews. In the middle of it all, Ferrari chairman, the charismatic and brilliant Luca di Montezemolo dropped in by helicopter from a meeting. Avoiding the press pack, he slipped into a waiting Lancia and was driven back to his office.

Then, without warning, the new Maserati 3200, which had just been launched in Paris, appeared to do a few laps of the circuit courtesy of an unknown test driver. Driving round immediately after a Formula One car is not a good idea. While undoubtedly beautiful with stunning lines and a delightful roar, the Maserati 3200 looks like it has the speed of a Ford Mondeo compared to the frisky prancing horse with its V10 engine and its ability to break late into the corners. But Schumacher was captivated and as soon as his television interviews had finished he was whisked away to try a Maserati in the factory.

Just before he departed, he spied an even more delightful toy – a Jaguar XK8 that was parked by the race track, ready to be put through its paces in comparison to the new Maserati. To the horror of the Ferrari management, Schumacher lurched towards this new toy eager to try it out. Just before disaster struck and a picture of a smiling Schumacher in a Jaguar was beamed around the world, the favoured one was told in no uncertain terms that this was one toy that was most definitely out of bounds. He was quickly bundled into the waiting Lancia 'people carrier' and despatched to meet the waiting chairman and the new Maserati.

Schumacher is not the only member of Ferrari who is constantly in demand both by the team and by the world's press. As Ross Brawn explains, 'Everyone is working seven days a week, at least 12 hours a day. It's an awkward time of year because we're very busy with the new car. It's the dilemma of picking the right priorities. We have a very hectic test programme. We are testing for three days at Fiorano, then next week we take two cars to Mugello, then the following week we have one car at Mugello, and one car at Fiorano. We are working on things that will give us an increased performance at Suzuka, like chassis changes, tyres, engine...'

Paolo Martinelli, the director of Engines, admitted that Ferrari was having to bring its development programme forward a month. Instead of the new changes being ready at the end of November for the new car, they needed to be ready for the end of October for the old car and the last race. This meant everyone was stretched. Never had Jean Todt's diplomatic and protective powers been more needed. The French Ferrari team boss is like a sponge. He absorbs all the external pressures, like the media and overly excitable Fiat shareholders, and keeps everyone away from his boys. He is highly protective of his team. 'I don't want people from outside to touch my people. I want to protect them. If something goes wrong, it is my responsibility to deal with it, not anyone else's.'

Todt is very balanced. As he says, 'We're still the same team whether we win or lose. When we win we're not heroes, and when we lose we're not good-for-nothings. There has to be a balance. I have to make sure the team is always in the best condition to do the job. We always try and move forward and make progress together.'

Inspite of the general downturn in the world economy, Todt is very positive about the future of Formula One. 'Even though the world economic situation is not good, Formula One is still very popular. Getting involved with Ferrari and Formula One is a great opportunity for companies. The big car manufacturers like Honda, Ford and BMW are all involved. There is a fascination with Formula One that makes the battle more difficult, but we've never had so many television viewers and Formula One is riding on the crest of a wave. I think companies get involved with a high profile international sport like Formula One to show the world they still have confidence. Being in Formula One gives you a strong position; it's the right time to attack, not give up.'

I wished Schumacher would give up whatever it was he was doing and come and talk to me. I'd been waiting for hours for an interview, but help was at hand in the form of Nigel Stepney. Schumacher is known as a workaholic, which is good for the team, up to a point. 'It's hard to tell a driver he's tired. Sometimes it's better to give a driver a break, than keep on pushing him all the time. They need a break, the same as any of the guys do. When they start getting nervous and agitated that is the time to take a couple of days off. It's better to take time off now, so everyone is ready for the pressures of the race.'

Any chance of Schumacher taking a break? 'Michael Schumacher at Ferrari is under a constant spotlight. He does learn, but if he makes a mistake it's made more out of than if, say, [Ricardo] Rosset makes a mistake. He's only human. He's not a computer, although he might be close to it.' Nigel Stepney laughed. 'He's close to a robot... but thankfully he's not one!'

Finally, it's proved that good things come to those who wait, and eventually I walked into Enzo Ferrari's old house, which had become Schumacher's headquarters for the duration of his stay. I popped in to see him in the room that is the centre of Ferrari's history: Enzo Ferrari's meeting room with the walls full of pictures from the old days — Fangio, Ascari, Villeneuve, Mansell and now Schumacher and Irvine. Schumi was deep in conversation with a man, seemingly discussing how to cut up balaclavas. I wondered if Ferrari was off to Suzuka or about to mount an armed robbery on Adrian Newey's office. Talking of whom, wouldn't he be the icing on the cake at Ferrari? Brawn, Byrne and Newey, what a combination. For the last few years it's been Schuey vs Newey. Wouldn't it be better to have the acclaimed aerodynamicist at Ferrari?

Schumacher pondered the question. 'It's true that wherever he's been over the last five or six years, he's created a good car. Whether it's only him is the question. McLaren has quite a big infrastructure. He was just one part of the chain that was missing to make it a complete package. It's difficult to quantify his job. I don't think there's any reason to have him here. I think we have a good group of people. We started off missing something on the aerodynamics of our car, but I don't think that's true now.'

Schumacher is reticent about stating exactly what is missing from the car. He will only say, 'We know what is missing and what we have to do to put it right. I believe a similar thing happened at McLaren. They had four or five bad years before the missing part was introduced, and now they're right on track.'

Schumacher believes Ferrari is now in the position of being right on track. 'We're now in that position and in my view we will be able to build a much better car. We've done a good job this year, but there's more room to use the new rules that were introduced last year to make a better car in 1999.'

Unlike most of Ferrari he doesn't think success is all down to him. 'Definitely not, I would say its 50/50. You can't say I'm more important than the car; we are both important in the general equation.'

So what's his view of 1998? 'We started low and Brazil was disappointing. We thought we were back with the win in Argentina, but it was in Montreal that we had good tyres and got up to speed. The tyre companies have picked up enormously and the competition of having two companies helps make improvements, and that's where we gain the most time.'

Everyone talks about pressure and stress. But Schumacher exudes the same, cool, focused presence whatever the situation. Is there a secret or is it part of his character? Like many of his colleagues Schumacher is a graduate of the famous Willy Dungl clinic. Dungl pioneered the psychological approach of relaxing and switching off when under extreme pressure. Schumacher was already cool and calculating, but the clinic still helped him. 'There was still something to learn about myself when I was there with Willy Dungl. Now it's so automatic that I don't purposely do anything to help me relax. If I feel I have to relax I do it automatically as it is part of me. I don't have any particular relaxation exercises, except breathing to calm down. I sometimes do this in the race if I feel the pressure.'

It's not true that Schumacher thinks of nothing else except racing on race day. As he says, 'Throughout the weekend I'm fairly relaxed. I might be with sponsors, or chatting to friends. My concentration comes naturally when I get in the car.'

Back at the factory the midnight oil was still burning. It's nine o'clock and Jean Todt is still thinking about the race at Suzuka. It's a good circuit for Ferrari as the drivers can make a difference. But it could all hinge on strategy. 'Sometimes you have to take risks. We had the same kind of strategy at Monaco as we did in Hungary, and yet it didn't work in Monaco as Michael had an accident with Wurz. In Hungary it worked, but if it hadn't worked everyone would have said were mad. I have to try and make sure we're in the best position to do the job now and in the future.'

Todt has no time to miss Paris. When he has a spare weekend he goes home, but right now he was too busy plotting the race and making sure of the future. Upstairs in his office,

Chief Designer Rory Byrne was thinking of the future and next year's car, as well as still fine-tuning this year's. It's a dual role that isn't easy. Inspite of being with Schumacher at Benetton he denies designing a car specifically for a driver. 'We don't design the car specifically for a particular driver. It's just that there were several fundamental design shortcomings in the 648 [last year's car] which we addressed. Eddie's done a lot of testing and contributed a lot to the overall test programme, above all on tyre testing. Test driver Luca Badoer has also done a lot of system testing, and a lot of preparatory work for the drivers to optimize. It's important to have a car everyone is happy with, not just the Number One driver.'

Both wind tunnels, the old and the new, are up and running, which is a tremendous bonus for the design team. They can have two aerodynamics teams working on the car, one in the old tunnel and one in the new, which is better suited for detailed work and for working on areas that are sensitive to size and speed.

Rory was also burning the midnight oil. 'We are flat out on developing the new car, and we have a huge development programme for this month before we go to Suzuka. I am very much involved in both programmes, as at the end of the day, the performance improvements we find for the last race will be carried over to the new car. We are optimizing the aerodynamic downforce for Japan, which is a medium speed track. We are also doing suspension work. Suzuka is fairly hard on tyres so we'll be using a harder compound than normal. Goodyear is very committed and we are working very hard to win in Japan.'

Ian Galliard at Shell was also busy on fuel. The fuel regulations undergo quite a radical change next year. 'We have to implement fuel regulations that will be European specifications by the year 2000. These require lower fuel emissions. There will be a new emission limit in 2000, and FIA is bringing the regulations in one year earlier in 1999. We have already supplied the new fuel to Ferrari. In fact we had the first batch ready in March. This means that Ferrari can get the best optimization for next year.'

For Ferrari and its partners it has been an exciting if nerve-wracking year. Edward Asprey has been close to the team for the three years that his company has been an official sponsor, but he is not jaded by the thrill of being close to the most glamorous team in Formula One. 'We still get a tremendous buzz from being in the garage with the team. We've had three magical, outstanding years with Ferrari. It's given us an enormous advantage for us to be able to take our clients to see "our" team. Win, lose or draw there is no other team like Ferrari. If all the teams changed but there was still Ferrari, Formula One would carry on as normal, but if all the other teams stayed the same and Ferrari withdrew, I don't believe Formula One would survive. Ferrari simply *is* Formula One.'

Long into the night the lights were still on at the Fiorano factory. Chief Press Officer Claudio Berro was buried under a pile of interview requests and faxes asking for information on Ferrari. His job is to act as an interface between the team and the media. It isn't easy. 'After Monza we had 220 pages of press cuttings. It just gets bigger. There is no other team that is as big as Ferrari or that holds such international interest. Now we have to prepare for the interest at Suzuka.'

● ● ●

Ah yes, Suzuka. The final showdown between the silver arrows and the prancing horse would take place on the other side of the world. In the end there could only be one winner. Would victory finally return to Ferrari?

CHAPTER FIFTEEN

The Final Countdown

'I believe that the work of the last few
weeks has paid off. I'm glad for the team
that they have made the improvements.
But today is only about qualifying.
Tomorrow is the race.'

Michael Schumacher,
*before the final Grand Prix
of the 1998 season*

Suzuka 1998. Action replay of 1997. Ferrari is one of two teams in contention for the Drivers' Championship and the Constructors' Championship. The five weeks between the Luxembourg Grand Prix at the Nurburgring and the last race of the season in Japan have passed in a whirl of testing, testing and more testing. Tyres, chassis, brakes, engine, wings, a new seat for Irvine – nothing has been left to chance. As he arrived at the circuit, Schumacher declared that he was on 'a difficult mission, but not an impossible one'.

Finally, it was time for the talking to stop and the action to begin. During Friday's practice session, Schumacher was fastest – but that's not always an accurate indicator of how things will turn out. Some teams were running on new tyres, some on full tanks, some with race set-up, some for fast qualifying times.

During Saturday's qualifying session, it seemed that Schumacher had the psychological advantage over Mika Hakkinen. Cool and collected, the German stood at the back of his garage while Hakkinen claimed provisional pole ten minutes into the session.

Another ten minutes later, Schumacher climbed into his car and drove onto the track to beat the time that Hakkinen had set. By the final sector he was an overall 3/10ths of a second faster. The champion-in-waiting was on provisional pole. The McLaren garage was visibly deflated, the Ferrari garage led by Chairman Luca di Montezemolo visibly elated.

However, the qualifying session had yet to be completed. Hakkinen responded by trying to better Schumacher's time, but he was still second fastest. Then, some 40 minutes into the session, Schumacher left the pits to give a demonstration of how it should be done. He put 6/10ths of a second between himself and the Finn, and pole position was Ferrari's. Hakkinen's team-mate, David Coulthard, was third with Eddie Irvine fourth. The dream situation – Ferrari, McLaren, McLaren, Ferrari on the first two rows of the grid. All was set for the final countdown. Schumacher declared himself happy with the session. 'I've been confident in the car all weekend. I have a good set up and I believe that the work of the last few weeks has paid off. I'm glad for the team that they have made the improvements. But today is only about qualifying. Tomorrow is the race.'

And never a truer word spoken! This was a race that was not only about the battle between Hakkinen and Schumacher, but also about the role of their respective team-mates, David Coulthard and Eddie Irvine. With Hakkinen having a 4-point advantage over Schumacher in the Drivers' Championship, and McLaren having a 15-point lead in the Constructors' competition, it was obvious that Coulthard's role would not be nearly as critical as Irvine's.

Since the Nurburgring when the Irishman had been criticized for supposedly letting Hakkinen pass him too easily, Irvine had been under pressure. He wasn't helped by the rumours that if he didn't perform well Jean Alesi was ready to step into his shoes.

In the event it was not only unfair — after all, Irvine is in the 'best drivers after Schumacher' category — but completely without foundation. Within the Ferrari camp, Irvine had always performed as he was expected to and refrained from whingeing, whereas the Berger-Alesi era had been fraught with arguments and complaints from both drivers. Ferrari would be mad to look backwards and not forwards, and the team knew this better than anyone else.

THE DREAM IS OVER
LUCA DI MONTEZEMOLO WAS CRUSHED

Everything looked set for a thrilling race — that is until the good luck gods decided otherwise. The warm-up lap was underway. Then the start of the race — aborted due to Jarno Trulli stalling his Prost. Another wait. Another warm-up lap. The second start to the race. Aborted due to ... Schumacher stalling. No! Horror on the faces of the Ferrari crew. It wasn't possible. This was one problem they really hadn't expected. As Jean Todt said: 'It's never happened before, in all the hours — weeks, in fact — of testing, we have never experienced the problem we had with Schumacher's car.'

That problem was a simple electrical fault on the clutch, which failed to open when Schumacher put the car in first gear. In effect, it ended all his hopes of winning the Drivers' Championship for he had to take the third start from the back of the grid. True, he went like a bullet out of the barrel of a gun and by the end of lap 2 he had moved up ten places to 10th position. But Hakkinen was in the lead — just what Ferrari didn't need, despite Irvine being right behind him. By lap 3 Schumacher was ninth, but Hakkinen answered by recording the fastest lap of the race so far. On lap 4, Irvine was close to Hakkinen, but not close enough to challenge for the lead.

By lap 19 Schumi was fifth. But then he came up against Damon Hill. Schumacher Junior, Hill's team-mate, had let Schumacher Senior past, but Damon wasn't playing ball. As Ralf later said: 'The team called Damon three times to let Michael past, but he didn't.' What a surprise!

By lap 30, once the major contenders had completed their first pit stops, Schumacher was lying in third place. But two laps later his championship aspirations disappeared when his right rear tyre blew. It was a long walk back to the pits.

Montezemolo was crushed by the blow. 'Our dream is over. It's a very sad moment for us, but I want to congratulate my team; we've had our best season for 20 years and we will win next year.' Contributing towards that success has been

Schumacher's stalwart team-mate Eddie Irvine. No one could have done more as the team's Number Two driver, and as he has done so many times during the season, he fulfilled the team's expectations at Suzuka by taking second place.

Schumacher himself seemed resigned to his fate rather than angry. He returned to the garage, changed into his jeans and a sweatshirt, and went to sit on the pit wall, where he was comforted by Jean Todt.

As Mika Hakkinen, winner at Suzuka and, more crucially, winner of the FIA 1998 Drivers' Championship by some 14 points, stepped out of his car at the end of the race, Schumacher was one of the first to congratulate him – despite his own feelings. Not only had he lost the Drivers' Championship, but Ferrari had to settle for second in the Constructors' Championship some 23 points behind McLaren.

Afterwards Schumacher said: 'At the end of the day we did a good job. We didn't lose the championship here, we lost it at the beginning of the year. Next year is another year. The world's still going around; we're still alive.'

A bit different from the raving, uncontrollable beast after the incident at Spa, although no one should underestimate Schumacher's bitter disappointment.

A QUESTION OF FAITH
WHEN WILL FERRARI BE BLESSED?

If there's luck to be had, it doesn't seem to be going Ferrari's way. Umberto Agnelli, brother of Fiat Boss, Gianni, declared: 'Michael Schumacher should take a trip to Lourdes, and then maybe we will be blessed. But in any case the team did a great job and it's never easy to play for everything at the final Grand Prix. It's a shame, as Schumacher pushed hard and drove a great race.'

Gianni Agnelli was also impressed with the teamwork, but thought the competition was just too strong. 'It was like finding Mike Tyson in front of us,' he said.

So what about next year? Will the 1998 Champions of Formula One, McLaren-Mercedes, win again? Is the team's brilliant aerodynamicist, Adrian Newey (who won the Championship when he was at Williams in 1997, before joining McLaren in 1998) too hard an act to beat? When will Ferrari win that elusive title? Luca di Montezemolo insists it will be in 1999. For Ferrari, next year has to be a winning year. Even the normally reticent Jean Todt is in agreement with his chairman: 'I feel it's the right time to promise the Championship next year. There won't be any excuses like tyres or anything else.'

Nineteen-ninety-nine has to be the winning year. In spite of the 'oh well, never mind' attitude that the team put on in public, in private they were devastated. Schumacher had promised the fans he would win the title within three years and he hadn't. He felt it was a personal failure. 'When I came to Ferrari I promised the fans I'd bring the World Championship back to them in three years, but unfortunately, I failed. I'm sorry, but I also want to ask the fans to stay close to Ferrari and believe in us.'

As Nigel Stepney said earlier in the year, 'We have to be ready at the beginning of the season'. And that's the key. Ferrari spent the first half of the season catching up. In Melbourne the McLarens were far superior to anyone else. Schumacher won in Argentina because the McLarens didn't run well. It was Canada and almost midway through the season, before the components of tyres, engine and aerodynamics started to come right. As we saw in France, there were a lot of modifications and Ferrari clearly took a step forward and offered McLaren a run for their money. But it didn't last.

After the victory at Silverstone, the results for Ferrari at Zeltweg and Hockenheim were disappointing. Spa was a disaster, a certain victory lost in a split second of inadvisable behaviour on the part of David Coulthard, and hot headedness on the part of Schumacher. Monza gave us all a glimmer of hope. The Nurburgring brought us all down to earth, and Suzuka just confirmed what we had all been thinking – McLaren were the best team.

Rory Byrne has now got a strong design and research team. The new wind tunnel at Maranello has been operational for a couple of months. This allows for intricate and detailed aerodynamic work to be done on a half size or full size car. This will make a tremendous difference. Cars today are about engines, aerodynamics and tyres. The V10 engine is excellent, the aerodynamics side will be much enhanced by the wind tunnel. That leaves the tyres. And that should even out as all the cars will be on Bridgestone tyres for the next season.

By the Tuesday after the race, 1998 had been consigned to the dustbin and the team were hard at work for 1999. Along with the majority of teams, Ferrari stayed in Japan for a tyre test. Goodyear has departed from Formula One; next season everyone will be on Bridgestone tyres. Of course, some of the teams, including McLaren, had already spent a full season racing on Bridgestone tyres, and McLaren might feel it has a head start for 1999 – but in Formula One nothing can be counted on.

On the Thursday before the race, Luca di Montezemolo and Jean Todt met the Chairman of Bridgestone, Yoichiro Kaizaki in Tokyo to discuss tyres. And the meeting went very well. 'Thanks to the excellent relationship between Bridgestone and Ferrari for the road cars, contact between the two companies has got off to a very good start.'

Next year the playing fields will be pretty level, as Ross Brawn said after the Nurburgring. After all, Ferrari might not be World Champions this year, but it has something that McLaren will never have – real power throughout the world. And there's nowhere else in the world where power counts as much as it does in Formula One.

So can Schumacher put the disappointment of 1998 behind him and think about the Drivers' and Constructors' Championships for the forthcoming season? 'We have to go for it next year,' he says. Then there's a slow smile. 'I *know* we're going to win next year.'

Race Results

THE 1998 FORMULA 1 WORLD CHAMPIONSHIP

8 March, Round 1: AUSTRALIA – Melbourne, 58 laps, 191.118 miles/ 307.574 km

1	Mika Hakkinen (McLaren MP4/13-Mercedes-Benz)	1h 31m 45.996s
2	David Coulthard (McLaren MP4/13-Mercedes-Benz)	1h 31m 46.698s
3	Heinz-Harald Frentzen (Williams FW20-Mecachrome)	57 laps
4	Eddie Irvine (Ferrari F300)	57 laps
5	Jacques Villeneuve (Williams FW20-Mecachrome)	57 laps
6	Johnny Herbert (Sauber C17-Petronas)	57 laps

(Pole Position: M Hakkinen, 1m 30.010s, 131.791 mph/ 212.096 km/h)
(Fastest lap: M Hakkinen, 1m 31.649s, 129.434 mph/ 208.303 km/h)
(Most laps led: M Hakkinen, 37)
M Schumacher (Ferrari F300) retired after 5 laps (engine)
Points – Drivers: Hakkinen 10, Coulthard 6, Frentzen 4, Irvine 3, Villeneuve, 2, Herbert 1.
Constructors: McLaren 16, Williams 6, Ferrari 3.

29 March, Round 2: BRAZIL – Interlagos, 72 laps, 192.019 miles/ 309.024 km

1	Mika Hakkinen (McLaren MP4/13-Mercedes-Benz)	1h 37m 11.747s
2	David Coulthard (McLaren MP4/13-Mercedes-Benz)	1h 37m 12.849s
3	Michael Schumacher (Ferrari F300)	1h 38m 12.297s
4	Alexander Wurz (Benetton B198-Playlife)	1h 38m 19.200s
5	Heinz-Harald Frentzen (Williams FW20-Mecachrome)	71 laps
6	Giancarlo Fisichella (Benetton B198-Playlife)	71 laps

(Pole Position: M Hakkinen, 1m 17.092s, 124.539 mph/ 200.425 km/h)
(Fastest lap: M Hakkinen, 1m 19.337s, 121.015 mph/ 194.754 km/h)
(Most laps led: M Hakkinen, 72)
E Irvine (Ferrari F300) finished 8th (71 laps)
Points – Drivers: Hakkinen 20, Coulthard 12, Frentzen 6, M Schumacher 4, Irvine & Wurz 3.
Constructors: McLaren 32, Williams 8, Ferrari 7.

12 April, Round 3: ARGENTINA – Buenos Aires, 72 laps, 190.419 miles/ 306.449 km

1	Michael Schumacher (Ferrari F300)	1h 48m 36.175s
2	Mika Hakkinen (McLaren MP4/13-Mercedes-Benz)	1h 48m 59.073s
3	Eddie Irvine (Ferrari F300)	1h 49m 33.920s
4	Alexander Wurz (Benetton B198-Playlife)	1h 49m 44.309s
5	Jean Alesi (Sauber C17-Petronas)	1h 49m 54.461s
6	David Coulthard (McLaren MP4/13-Mercedes-Benz)	1h 49m 55.926s

(Pole Position: D Coulthard, 1m 25.852s, 110.971 mph/ 178.591 km/h)
(Fastest lap: A Wurz, 1m 28.179s, 108.043 mph/ 173.878 km/h)
(Most laps led: M Schumacher, 54)
Points – Drivers: Hakkinen 26, M Schumacher 14, Coulthard 13, Irvine 7, Frentzen & Wurz 6.
Constructors: McLaren 39, Ferrari 21, Williams 8.

26 April, Round 4: SAN MARINO – Imola, 62 laps, 189.794 miles/ 305.443 km

1	David Coulthard (McLaren MP4/13-Mercedes-Benz)	1h 34m 24.593s
2	Michael Schumacher (Ferrari F300)	1h 34m 29.147s
3	Eddie Irvine (Ferrari F300)	1h 35m 16.368s
4	Jacques Villeneuve (Williams FW20-Mecachrome)	1h 35m 19.183s
5	Heinz-Harald Frentzen (Williams FW20-Mecachrome)	1h 35m 42.069s
6	Jean Alesi (Sauber C17-Petronas)	61 laps

(Pole Position: D Coulthard, 1m 25.973s, 128.274 mph/ 206.437 km/h)
(Fastest lap: M Schumacher, 1m 29.345s, 123.433 mph/ 198.646 km/h)
(Most laps led: D Coulthard, 62)
Points – Drivers: Hakkinen 26, Coulthard 23, M Schumacher 20, Irvine 11, Frentzen 8, Wurz 6.
Constructors: McLaren 49, Ferrari 31, Williams 13.

10 May, Round 5: SPAIN – Montmelo, 65 laps, 190.883 miles/ 307.196 km

1	Mika Hakkinen (McLaren MP4/13-Mercedes-Benz)	1h 33m 37.621s
2	David Coulthard (McLaren MP4/13-Mercedes-Benz)	1h 33m 47.060s
3	Michael Schumacher (Ferrari F300)	1h 34m 24.716s
4	Alexander Wurz (Benetton B198-Playlife)	1h 34m 40.159s
5	Rubens Barrichello (Stewart SF-2 -Ford Cosworth)	64 laps
6	Jacques Villeneuve (Williams FW20-Mecachrome)	64 laps

(Pole Position: M Hakkinen, 1m 20.262s, 131.771 mph/ 212.065 km/h)
(Fastest lap: M Hakkinen, 1m 24.275s, 125.497 mph/ 201.967 km/h)
(Most laps led: M Hakkinen, 63)
E Irvine (Ferrari F300) retired after 28 laps (accident)
Points – Drivers: Hakkinen 36, Coulthard 29, M Schumacher 24, Irvine 11, Wurz 9, Frentzen 8.
Constructors: McLaren 65, Ferrari 35, Williams 14.

24 May, Round 6: MONACO – Monte Carlo, 78 laps, 163.188 miles/ 262.626 km

1	Mika Hakkinen (McLaren MP4/13-Mercedes-Benz)	1h 51m 23.595s
2	Giancarlo Fisichella (Benetton B198-Playlife)	1h 51m 35.070s
3	Eddie Irvine (Ferrari F300)	1h 52m 04.973s
4	Mika Salo (Arrows A19-Arrows)	1h 52m 23.958s
5	Jacques Villeneuve (Williams FW20-Mecachrome)	77 laps
6	Pedro Diniz (Arrows A19-Arrows)	77 laps

(Pole Position: M Hakkinen, 1m 19.798s, 94.385 mph/ 151.899 km/h)
(Fastest lap: M Hakkinen, 1m 22.948s, 90.801 mph/ 146.130 km/h)
(Most laps led: M Hakkinen, 78)
M Schumacher (Ferrari F300) finished 10th (76 laps)
Points – Drivers: Hakkinen 46, Coulthard 29, M Schumacher 24, Irvine 15, Wurz 9,
Frentzen & Villeneuve 8.
Constructors: McLaren 75, Ferrari 39, Benetton & Williams 16.

7 June, Round 7: CANADA – Montreal, 69 laps, 189.549 miles/ 305.049 km

1	Michael Schumacher (Ferrari F300)	1h 40m 57.355s
2	Giancarlo Fisichella (Benetton B198-Playlife)	1h 41m 14.017s
3	Eddie Irvine (Ferrari F300)	1h 41m 57.414s
4	Alexander Wurz (Benetton B198-Playlife)	1h 42m 00.587s
5	Rubens Barrichello (Stewart SF-2-Ford Cosworth)	1h 42m 18.868s
6	Jan Magnussen (Stewart SF-2-Ford Cosworth)	68 laps

(Pole Position: D Coulthard, 1m 18.213s, 126.443 mph/ 203.490 km/h)

(Fastest lap: M Schumacher, 1m 19.379s, 124.586 mph/ 200.501 km/h)
(Most laps led: M Schumacher, 27)
Points – Drivers: Hakkinen 46, M Schumacher 34, Coulthard 29, Irvine 19, Fisichella 13, Wurz 12.
Constructors: McLaren 75, Ferrari 53, Benetton 25.

28 June, Round 8: FRANCE – Magny-Cours, 71 laps, 187.383 miles/ 301.564 km

1	Michael Schumacher (Ferrari F300)	1h 34m 45.026s
2	Eddie Irvine (Ferrari F300)	1h 35m 04.601s
3	Mika Hakkinen (McLaren MP4/13-Mercedes-Benz)	1h 35m 04.773s
4	Jacques Villeneuve (Williams FW20-Mecachrome)	1h 35m 51.991s
5	Alexander Wurz (Benetton B198-Playlife)	70 laps
6	David Coulthard (McLaren MP4/13-Mercedes-Benz)	70 laps

(Pole Position: M Hakkinen, 1m 14.929s, 126.880 mph/ 204.193 km/h)
(Fastest lap: D Coulthard, 1m 17.523s, 122.634 mph/ 197.361 km/h)
(Most laps led: M Schumacher, 70)
Points – Drivers: Hakkinen 50, M Schumacher 44, Coulthard 30, Irvine 25, Wurz 14,
Fisichella 13.
Constructors: McLaren 80, Ferrari 69, Benetton 27.

12 July, Round 9: BRITAIN – Silverstone, 60 laps, 191.566 miles/ 308.296 km

1	Michael Schumacher (Ferrari F300)	1h 47m 02.450s
2	Mika Hakkinen (McLaren MP4/13-Mercedes-Benz)	1h 47m 24.915s
3	Eddie Irvine (Ferrari F300)	1h 47m 31.649s
4	Alexander Wurz (Benetton B198-Playlife)	59 laps
5	Giancarlo Fisichella (Benetton B198-Playlife)	59 laps
6	Ralf Schumacher (Jordan 198-Mugen Honda)	59 laps

(Pole Position: M Hakkinen, 1m 23.271s, 138.078 mph/ 222.214 km/h)
(Fastest lap: M Schumacher, 1m 35.704s, 120.140 mph/ 193.346 km/h)
(Most laps led: M Hakkinen, 50)
Points – Drivers: Hakkinen 56, M Schumacher 54, Coulthard 30, Irvine 29,
Wurz 17, Fisichella 15.
Constructors: McLaren 86, Ferrari 83, Benetton 32.
(note: M Schumacher originally awarded a 10 second penalty, but this was later
withdrawn)

26 July, Round 10: AUSTRIA – A1-Ring, 71 laps, 190.543 miles/ 306.649 km

1	Mika Hakkinen (McLaren MP4/13-Mercedes-Benz)	1h 30m 44.086s
2	David Coulthard (McLaren MP4/13-Mercedes-Benz)	1h 30m 49.375s
3	Michael Schumacher (Ferrari F300)	1h 31m 23.178s
4	Eddie Irvine (Ferrari F300)	1h 31m 28.062s
5	Ralf Schumacher (Jordan 198-Mugen Honda)	1h 31m 34.740s
6	Jacques Villeneuve (Williams FW20-Mecachrome)	1h 31m 37.288s

(Pole Position: G Fisichella, 1m 29.598s, 107.830 mph/ 173.535 km/h)
(Fastest lap: D Coulthard, 1m 12.878s, 132.569 mph/ 213.348 km/h)
(Most laps led: M Hakkinen, 69)
Points – Drivers: Hakkinen 66, M Schumacher 58, Coulthard 36, Irvine 32,
Wurz 17, Fisichella 15.
Constructors: McLaren 102, Ferrari 90, Benetton 32.

2 August, Round 11: GERMANY – Hockenheim, 45 laps, 190.783 miles/ 307.035 km

1   Mika Hakkinen (McLaren MP4/13-Mercedes-Benz)   1h 20m 47.984s
2   David Coulthard (McLaren MP4/13-Mercedes-Benz)   1h 20m 48.410s
3   Jacques Villeneuve (Williams FW20-Mecachrome)   1h 20m 50.561s
4   Damon Hill (Jordan 198-Mugen Honda)   1h 20m 55.169s
5   Michael Schumacher (Ferrari F300)   1h 21m 00.597s
6   Ralf Schumacher (Jordan 198-Mugen Honda)   1h 21m 17.722s
(Pole Position: M Hakkinen, 1m 41.838s, 149.872 mph/ 241.195 km/h)
(Fastest lap: D Coulthard, 1m 46.116s, 143.830 mph/ 231.471 km/h)
(Most laps led: M Hakkinen, 43)
E Irvine (Ferrari F300) finished 8th (1h 21m 19.633s)
Points – Drivers: Hakkinen 76, M Schumacher 60, Coulthard 42, Irvine 32,
Wurz 17, Villeneuve 16.
Constructors: McLaren 118, Ferrari 92, Benetton 32.

16 August, Round 12: HUNGARY – Hungaroring, 77 laps, 190.043 miles/ 305.844 km

1   Michael Schumacher (Ferrari F300)   1h 45m 25.550s
2   David Coulthard (McLaren MP4/13-Mercedes-Benz)   1h 45m 34.983s
3   Jacques Villeneuve (Williams FW20-Mecachrome)   1h 46m 09.994s
4   Damon Hill (Jordan 198-Mugen Honda)   1h 46m 20.626s
5   Heinz-Harald Frentzen (Williams FW20-Mecachrome)   1h 46m 22.060s
6   Mika Hakkinen (McLaren MP4/13-Mercedes-Benz)   76 laps
(Pole Position: M Hakkinen, 1m 16.973s, 115.432 mph/ 185.769 km/h)
(Fastest lap: M Schumacher, 1m 19.286s, 112.064 mph/ 180.350 km/h)
(Most laps led: M Hakkinen, 46)
E Irvine (Ferrari F300) retired after 13 laps (gearbox)
Points – Drivers: Hakkinen 77, M Schumacher 70, Coulthard 48, Irvine 32,
Villeneuve 20, Wurz 17.
Constructors: McLaren 125, Ferrari 102, Benetton 32.

30 August, Round 13: BELGIUM – Spa-Francorchamps, 44 laps, 190.498 miles/ 306.577 km

1   Damon Hill (Jordan 198-Mugen Honda)   1h 43m 47.407s
2   Ralf Schumacher (Jordan 198-Mugen Honda)   1h 43m 48.339s
3   Jean Alesi (Sauber C17-Petronas)   1h 43m 54.647s
4   Heinz-Harald Frentzen (Williams FW20-Mecachrome)   1h 44m 19.650s
5   Pedro Diniz (Arrows A19-Arrows)   1h 44m 39.089s
6   Jarno Trulli (Prost AP01-Peugeot)   42 laps
(Pole Position: M Hakkinen, 1m 48.682s, 143.418 mph/ 230.809 km/h)
(Fastest lap: M Schumacher, 2m 03.766s, 125.939 mph/ 202.679 km/h)
(Most laps led: D Hill, 26)
M Schumacher and E Irvine (Ferrari F300) both retired after 25 laps (accident)
Points – Drivers: Hakkinen 77, M Schumacher 70, Coulthard 48, Irvine 32,
Villeneuve 20, Wurz 17.
Constructors: McLaren 125, Ferrari 102, Williams 33.

13 September, Round 14: ITALY – Monza, 53 laps, 189.859 miles/ 305.548 km

1   Michael Schumacher (Ferrari F300)   1h 17m 09.672s
2   Eddie Irvine (Ferrari F300)   1h 17m 47.649s
3   Ralf Schumacher (Jordan 198-Mugen Honda)   1h 17m 50.824s

4 Mika Hakkinen (McLaren MP4/13-Mercedes-Benz) 1h 18m 05.343s
5 Jean Alesi (Sauber C17-Petronas) 1h 18m 11.544s
6 Damon Hill (Jordan 198-Mugen Honda) 1h 18m 16.360s
(Pole Position: M Schumacher, 1m 25.289s, 151.334 mph/ 243.548 km/h)
(Fastest lap: M Hakkinen, 1m 25.139s, 151.601 mph/ 243.977 km/h)
(Most laps led: M Schumacher, 34)
Points − Drivers: Hakkinen & M Schumacher 80, Coulthard 48, Irvine 38,
Villeneuve 20, Hill & Wurz 17.
Constructors: McLaren 128, Ferrari 118, Williams 33.

27 September, Round 15: LUXEMBOURG − Nurburgring, 67 laps, 189.664 miles/ 305.235 km
1 Mika Hakkinen (McLaren MP4/13-Mercedes-Benz) 1h 32m 14.789s
2 Michael Schumacher (Ferrari F300) 1h 32m 17.000s
3 David Coulthard (McLaren MP4/13-Mercedes-Benz) 1h 32m 48.952s
4 Eddie Irvine (Ferrari F300) 1h 33m 12.971s
5 Heinz-Harald Frentzen (Williams FW20-Mecachrome) 1h 33m 15.036s
6 Giancarlo Fisichella (Benetton B198-Playlife) 1h 33m 16.148s
(Pole Position: M Schumacher, 1m 18.561s, 129.727 mph/ 208.775 km/h)
(Fastest lap: M Hakkinen, 1m 20.450s, 126.681 mph/ 203.873 km/h)
(Most laps led: M Hakkinen, 43)
Points − Drivers: Hakkinen 90, M Schumacher 86, Coulthard 52, Irvine 41,
Villeneuve 20, Hill & Wurz 17.
Constructors: McLaren 142, Ferrari 127, Williams 35.

1 November, Round 16: JAPAN − Suzuka, 51 laps, 185.708miles/298.868km
1 Mike Hakkinen (McLaren MP4/13-Mercedes-Benz) 1h 27m 22.835s
2 Eddie Irvine (Ferrari F300) 1h 27m 29.026s
3 David Coulthard (McLaren MP4/13-Mercedes-Benz) 1h 27m 50.197s
4 Damon Hill (Jordan 198-Mugen Honda) 1h 28m 38.026s
5 Heinz-Harald Frentzen (Williams FW20-Mecachrome) 1h 28m 36.392s
6 Jacques Villeneuve (Williams FW20 Mecachrome) 1h 28m 38.402s
(Pole Position: M Schumacher, 1m 36.293s, 136.224 mph/ 219.231 km/h)
(Fastest lap: M Schumacher, 1m 40.190s, 130.925mph/ 210.704 km/h)
(Most laps led: M Hakkinen, 51)
M Schumacher (Ferrari F300) retired after 31 laps (rear puncture)
Final points − Drivers: Hakkinen 100, M Schumacher 86, Coulthard 56,
Irvine 47, Villeneuve 21, Hill 20.
Constructors: McLaren 156, Ferrari 133, Williams 38.

ACKNOWLEDGEMENTS

I would like to thank the following for their practical help and moral support: Ferrari past and present – Luca di Montezemolo, Jean Todt, Antonio Ghini, Giancarlo Baccini, Stefano Domenicali, Ross Brawn, Paolo Martinelli and the engine men, John Barnard, Vijay Kothary, Rory Byrne, Willem Toet, Gastav Brunner, Giorgio Ascanelli, Nigel Stepney and all the 'boys' including Ignazio Lunetta and Luca Baldisserri, the race engineers and, of course, Michael Schumacher and Eddie Irvine, Heiner Buchinger and Sonia Irvine. Three people have been exceptional in their support and commitment and without them this book would not have been written: Jackie Ireland of Shell, Claudio Berro of Ferrari, and Derick Allsop – friend and colleague. Other colleagues, including Stan Piecha and Roy Matts, have been ready with wine and song at the end of a hard day, while Roger Kelly is a great friend and much valued adviser. I must thank everyone at Shell for their professional attitude and outstanding technical expertise; also Chantal Cerruti, Edward Asprey and Rosalind Milani Gallieni; and Maurizio Arrivabene and his loyal team at Marlboro. At publishers CollinsWillow, Michael Doggart, Tom Whiting, Chris Stone, Jenny Macmillan and their respective teams have produced a wonderful book.

There are many other people I should thank, above all Geoffrey and Margaret Nottage, my parents and friends who are always by my side in joy and in sorrow; my Lynden Gate buddies, especially Liz Chisman – wife of Neil and mother of Abigail and Tom – who has always been there for me; Fiona Wilson, a good friend and intelligent adviser; Patrick and Heather Mayhew, who provided a safe harbour; Lizzi Capper, the blonde bombshell; Stephanie Moore, for her friendship and for helping me find my way in London; Father Vincent Cooper for attempting to keep me morally upright; Kate Maguire for helping me to be happy; Desmond Kelly for the Prozac; David and Maureen Royston-Lee, my godson Theo, and his sister Alice for their gift of deep and constant friendship; Jane Hamilton-Parker for her spiritual guidance and for being a wonderful friend who is always there for me; the legendary Ron, Reg and John; Trevor Mooney for looking after me and making sure my house and life never fall apart; Brian for keeping my house spotlessly clean, and Colin for transport and advice; Rebecca Spenser-Underhill for being a caring friend and picking me up when I'm down; Terry and Toots Venables for their friendship and sharing the good times and the bad; Jan Keetch for being lovely and caring as always; Dorrie Lang for her friendship and shared life experiences; Fiona Renfrew, my Australian buddy and long-time friend; Peter Lederer and his magnificent staff at The Gleneagles Hotel; Ross Duffield, a man who couldn't care less about Formula One but is a great estate manager; Rita, a passionate Michael Schumacher fan (may her dreams come true); Brian, with thanks for keeping a watchful eye on us all; and the wonderful Glenn Lyons, for offering me the hand of friendship when I needed it most.

PICTURE CREDITS

Ercole Colombo, Studio Colombo: Plate section pp 1–10(top)
Allsport Photographic: Plate section pp 11(centre, bottom)–16

THE CREATIVE TEAM

Text design by Graeme Andrew; cover design by Nik Keevil
Re-structured and edited for paperback by Sandra Stafford
Race statistics by David Hayhoe